ANSWERING YOUR CALL

Other books by John P. Schuster

Hum-Drum to Hot-Diggity: on Leadership

The Power of Open-book Management

The Open-book Management Fieldbook

Answering Your Call

A GUIDE TO

LIVING YOUR

DEEPEST

PURPOSE

John P. Schuster

BK
BERRETT-KOEHLER PUBLISHERS, INC.
San Francisco

Berrett-Koehler Publishers, Inc.
235 Montgomery Street, Suite 650
San Francisco, CA 94104-2916
Tel: (415) 288-0260 Fax: (415) 362-2512 www.bkconnection.com

Ordering Information

Quantity sales. Special discounts are available on quantity purchases by corpo-
rations, associations, and others. For details, contact the "Special Sales Department" at the Berrett-Koehler address above.

Individual sales. Berrett-Koehler publications are available through most bookstores. They can also be ordered direct from Berrett-Koehler: Tel: (800) 929-
2929; Fax: (802) 864-7626; www.bkconnection.com

Orders for college textbook/course adoption use. Please contact Berrett-Koehler:
Tel: (800) 929-2929; Fax: (802) 864-7626.

Orders by U.S. trade bookstores and wholesalers. Please contact Publishers Group West,
1700 Fourth Street, Berkeley, CA 94710. Tel: (510) 528-1444; Fax: (510) 528-3444.

Berrett-Koehler and the BK logo are registered trademarks of Berrett-Koehler
Publishers, Inc.

Printed in the United States of America

Berrett-Koehler books are printed on long-lasting acid-free paper. When it is
available, we choose paper that has been manufactured by environmentally
responsible processes. These may include using trees grown in sustainable
forests, incorporating recycled paper, minimizing chlorine in bleaching, or recy-
cling the energy produced at the paper mill.

Library of Congress Cataloging-in-Publication Data

Schuster, John P.
    Answering your call : a guide for living your deepest purpose /
by John P. Schuster.
        p. cm.
    Includes bibliographical references and index.
    ISBN 1-57675-205-4
    1. Conduct of life. 2. Vocation. I. Title.
BJ1595 .S42 2002
170´.443—dc21   2002028008

First Edition

08 07 06 05   10 9 8 7 6 5 4 3 2

Interior Design: Gopa & Ted2   Proofreader: Henrietta Bensussen
Copy Editor: Sandra Beris   Indexer: Do Mi Stauber
Production: Linda Jupiter, Jupiter Productions

This book is dedicated to

all the grand provocateurs and evocateurs who activated me: Sister Veronice of my Omaha grade school, Thomas Savage, S.J., at Xavier, Bill McGrane II in my twenties, Peter Block and Frederic Hudson in midlife.

And to the leaders who started careers in the marketplace, in government, and in community and who now transform them into calls.

Contents

Preface

A GOOD NUMBER of profound life guides and competent mentors have made themselves available to me in my life. As long as I can remember, I have been motivated to do good and live a meaningful life. Yet I often missed the signals of my calling. I dallied when I should have sprung forward; I lurched ahead when I should have delayed. I went for worldly goals and titles when I should have retreated from things material; I swore off worldly things when it was time to accept and use them.

I enjoyed a happy childhood with loving parents and only the usual traumas to endure. One of the world's great religions and its heritage absorbed me, giving me rituals to mark the passages of my life from childhood to adolescence to adulthood. I was afforded a well-balanced education in private schools with dedicated teachers setting high standards and taking the time to give me individual attention. I inherited the privileges of my culture. I am white, male, from a stable middle-class family and was bright enough to make the most of those educational opportunities, graduating from university *summa cum laude* and going on for my M.A. Many of my athletic coaches brought out the best in my team play and built my confidence for achieving difficult goals. My siblings were loving and attentive, and my extended family was a place of joy and acceptance for my life and the place it held in the loose clan of Schusters and Cunninghams that we remain to this day.

But in spite of these gifts and resources, a steady stream of available knowledge, and even wisdom, I blew it on numerous occasions. I did not always heed my calling. At times, life called me and I either refused to hear or created my own false signals so I could avoid the real choices and make more convenient ones. I muted the call entirely on occasion, or having heard it, responded from my ego needs and delusions and their hold on my life.

In my midtwenties, I escaped for a year into an intentional community that, when it was at its worst, played on fear, grandiosity, and apocalyptic views of the world, which made it a cult. Later on, for several years, I avoided telling the truth to myself about a failed marriage as routines, mutual fear, and two wonderful sons kept us bound together. I betrayed the marriage and myself in a series of questionable choices. In my thirties, though called to significant work, I gave seminars about time management and building prioritized to-do lists when the world needed deeper answers to far bigger questions about life and work contributions. In my forties, I refused to see the truth about my relationship with a business partner, colluded in a partial dysfunction for years, and ended this flawed relationship with legal moves because it was too late for the truth to be of any help.

Through it all, life has been rich and I have been blessed. I have given every day my best shot to stay heads-up and alert. I have tapped all the resources I was lucky enough to inherit and sought out more. I have read heaps of self-help and spiritual and leadership books, and gone to more than my share of seminars, workshops, and conventions. Through almost all of these years I have kept a journal, prayed, and meditated. I have thought about the meaning of life continually. I have taken occasional retreats to monasteries.

I have stayed true to my duties in the world and have been largely trustworthy, and when I haven't been, I have cleaned up after my messes. I have remained a devoted dad while living six hundred miles away from my two sons. My second marriage partner helps me stay on my path through her accumulated wisdom and love. The business I have created has allowed me considerable travel around the world, ample income, and most importantly, a sense of some contribution in a world that is in much need of better approaches to living our potential as individuals and organizations. I have become devoted to leadership development and increasing social capital inside enterprises and between them in communities. On many occasions I have been called to add value for an enterprise or support leaders in their work, and have done the job in front of me.

I have marched and stumbled ahead in a life of work and fun and sad-
ness, health and joy and sorrow, love and support and conflict, learning and study and illusions. I have kept moving, two steps forward, one
step back, always with the intention of pursuing my destiny and hoping I am listening to my life through the best parts of my self, religion,
family, and what is true in society. Once I got the insights that a call was
providing (although sometimes it was more like an order with no
insights attached), I tried to respond to the call as intelligently as I
could with enough courage to do what needed to be done.

I write this book because I assume I am not alone.

In fact, I believe I am typical of any person attempting to live a conscious life. As I look back on my own life, I want the book to provide
a helpful context for twenty-somethings with a clean life slate, for mid-
lifers dealing with the decisions of specializing careers and the mystify-
ing work and rewards of intimacy, and for elders looking at the years
that remain. It is for all people on the path of a purposeful life who are
attempting to answer the sequence of calls they experience with as few
delays, setbacks, mistakes, and moral failings as possible. With all the
gifts and resources I inherited and absorbed, I could have used more—
an insight or a tip here, a reminder there, a model or a story or inspi-
rational example to help me on my way.

Although my experience in making the right and wrong decisions
has been helpful, using my life examples and reflections as the only
source for this book would be too limiting. Accordingly, I tapped the
lessons of history and literature, and I asked many others whom I
admire for the intention with which they live what they learned on their
way about callings. You'll meet several of them throughout *Answering
Your Call*. From their reports, they, like you and I, have learned some
lessons about calls the hard way, while others they eased into.

May your decisions concerning the calls to which you are responding summon the very best of you for the good of us all and for future
generations. My hope is that this book will help you on your way.

John Schuster
September 2002
Kansas City, Missouri

Introduction

You Are Called

THE RESOUNDING MESSAGE from the great religions for millennia, and from psychology more recently, is the same: humans aren't happy consuming and pursuing creature comforts, although many of us give it a good try. Only by discovering, and then somehow creatively deploying, our unique combination of gifts, can we ever feel the deep satisfaction of a life well lived.

I agree that human creativity and lasting value is possible only when individuals determine to address some problem, advance some knowledge, or serve a cause or humanity in some fashion. When they do this they are answering a call to do something that matters. They have purpose and are out to make a difference. They choose significance over success.

The flip side of doing something that matters is doing something that doesn't. It is sitting on our duffs and doing whatever we feel like and having no intention of adding value. Yes, there is a time for resting and vegging out. The world only gets better, however, if a good number of us decide to add value.

So there is good news here.

For various reasons, a large number of humans seem wired to serve and build and solve in order to feel that their lives count. This creates a happy alignment between what the world needs and what many individuals feel compelled to do. Answering a call affects individual states of well-being and has a lot to do with the state of the world.

If you don't agree with the ideas up to this point, if you don't think there is really any such thing as a call, then you are likely not to benefit from this book. If you agree with the notion that calls are central to our existence and well-being and you'd like to explore this phenomenon more completely, then you've come to the right place.

DIFFICULTIES OF THE CALL

For all the agreement on the importance of calls, we see little guidance on how to answer them as they come in their many forms throughout our lives. This book is meant to further the discussion on what calls are and how people can work with them.

In preparation for this book, I sent a series of questions to people who I consider are living authentic lives of adding value. I did not ask them ahead of time if they related to the idea of being called in their lives, but the many who responded obviously did. You'll meet some of them in the book, and learn about the joys and challenges of their personal experience. They will pop up to support a theory with a lived experience or to articulate a key concept in a way that adds dimensions and textures to the principles.

Many of the people who wrote down their thoughts for this book, and many hundreds more whom I've worked with over years of consulting and coaching, report on the difficulties of managing their lives within this sense of being called.

These are some of the key questions they ask of themselves:

- Am I really hearing the call or is it something else, like wishful thinking, that's at work?
- If I am responding to the call, why do I still have times of doubt?
- Why does it seem to take so long to discover your call?

- Is it possible to have more than one calling in a lifetime, or even operating at the same time, pulling you in different directions?
- How do I best handle those who seem to want to squelch my desire to live a called life?
- What do I do if I am the one doing the squelching?

A modern novelist, Doris Lessing, found an imaginative way to describe the difficulties of perceiving a call in her book *Briefing for a Descent into Hell.*[1] In this novel, the "briefing" is what God gives us before our birth into our bodies, our soul's descent into flesh. But after our births we remember the briefing only dimly, because taking on a body weakens the ability of the spirit to remember who we are and what we are here for. So the nagging sense of having forgotten something important, the longing without cause, the calls that haunt us like whispers from a little too far away, come from our remembering parts and fragments of the briefing. The calling is not forgotten entirely, but it is muted and fuzzy, like a distant radio station whose signal is filled with static.

There are stories—and you may have heard some personally—of people who have a clear sense of a call since they were young. They focus on the pursuit of a dream, and rising above or with circumstances, achieve notable success by making the dream happen.

This book, however, is more about the many of us who don't make the headlines with our stellar achievements. We have a sense of purpose much of the time, but we achieve less notable results than the stars in the field who have obvious outstanding gifts. Although a call is sometimes clear, it can often feel like a dimly remembered dream that won't become clear, no matter how much we think about it.

MULTIPLE CALLS

Some would assert that the call is a figment of an overworked imagination. Since you can't touch or weigh a call, for these thinkers such things must not exist. We will address these thinkers simply—we will ignore them. As you read this, you may or may not be at a time in your life when the sense of calling is operative. But at some time, and perhaps several times, you have likely had that experience, or if *you* haven't, you have watched others living deeply on purpose who have. That is enough proof for us.

So we start from the premise that there is such a thing, and we spend our time exploring the forms that calls take, why it is difficult to live them, and how we may go about the thinking and decisions and tasks that go into doing that well.

We make a common mistake when we think of *a* call, the big kahuna of calls, the call of all calls, that will provide direction and meaning for a lifetime. Again, this may happen for some. But more likely for most of us, our callings will take many shapes, some quite different from others we have lived previously. A calling "to do the most good in the world I can" is a good one, but when you live in Akron, Ohio, and you are in your twenties starting your career as a reporter, this calling looks a lot different than it does twenty years later when you are a journalism professor at Yale.

Paul Anderson, a coach and consultant in the Bay Area, confirms that the "one true big call frame" was not helpful to him. "It is only in recent years . . . that I came to believe in my calling. What hindered me was my initial belief that a calling was like Paul on the road to Damascus—flashy—and that we are called to a specific job."

Having *a* calling may mean having a lifelong, somewhat specific purpose that draws you into roles in a clear progression. Colin Powell goes from soldier to colonel to general to Secretary of State. Good for him and others like him. But such a clean script, an obviously progressive set of steps, is not for all of us by any means. More of us go from starting a career in sales, for example, to becoming a devoted parent when raising our kids takes precedence over everything, to becoming a leader in our church while we work at the local chamber of commerce. Our roles combine and have equal weight—parenting for twenty-five years is as important, or more important, than the business career we build and like or even love for the most part.

Our roles, as spouse, as businessperson, are the "way we show up in the world," as developmentalist Frederic Hudson puts it, and each role can have its own deep purpose, depending both on how we view it and how much of ourselves we pour into it.[2] Although each may constitute a calling worthy of such involvement, they can both operate at the same time, generate the same passion simultaneously. Being called to becoming a loving devoted parent coincides with serving customers in a way that delights them and enlivens their spirit.

So I am of the school, and this book has the point of view, that you can have several callings in a lifetime, that you need to balance and combine them, respond to them in a creative fashion, renew them and rediscover them with growing sets of roles and skills. And yes, there may be a constant thread through the callings in your life, but you may also have disjointed chapters and blind alleys that leave you stumped as to their commonality. Calls can work like that too.

SOURCES OF THE CALL

What the source of these callings is could be a very lengthy discussion—too lengthy and too philosophical for our purposes. But a few angles on the question may be helpful.

Many would put it very simply: the call is God talking to you.

The theology and belief system of these people is such that no further interpretation is needed. When you are trying to discern what decision to make, you are trying to hear what God has in store for you. Prayer is the process we use for our dialogue with the divine, and if we pray sincerely and develop discernment we can align our wills with the will of God.

I will use a theological position occasionally in this book, but not predominantly. Although this God-position holds great meaning for me and many others, including those who responded to my questions for this book, other ways of talking about callings are also useful.

Those who are less theologically and more psychologically inclined would say that the call is your higher self sending you a message about what you should be doing. This explanation rests on the belief that humans have a variety of drives and urges, and the one that should be in charge of our most important decisions is our highest will, our self, a seat of wisdom and guidance that constitutes the most advanced part of our psyche. We have a built-in psychological drive to grow to our fullest potential and extend and expand our faculties for living. This drive takes on a voice and we must heed this voice of self to make anything meaningful out of our lives.

Those who are biologically rooted in their thinking offer a third explanation: our brain cells need stimulation or they shrivel up under the routine of life. So the call and its urges and voices are sets of neurons stretching themselves out for new stimulation, the kind that comes from new challenges. As we learn to feed our brains, we can, if we work at it, take on lifelong learning habits that keep our brains and our lives growing. Our neurology drives us to grow into the next set of projects to accomplish and knowledge to master. If our brain stem takes care of our safety need and our limbic system or midbrain is the source of our emotions, then the will to move ahead in life is located elsewhere.

Our frontal lobes in particular are the culprits responsible for the calling urge. It is the part of our brain where we will ourselves to the next level, where we envision a better world that we can help make come about.

Jonas Salk spoke of the parts of our brain that drove evolution and growth versus the parts devoted to survival and competition. He urged us to heed the former so we could create lives of service.

A fourth angle on the sources of calls is sociological: the call is the part of society and your upbringing that you have coded into your own internal messages saying, *"Yoo hoo! Wake up and get on with your life."* From this perspective, the call is the collection of social messages from parents and teachers and others we have looked up to that we have incorporated into our own values and made our own. According to this explanation, our conscience and a set of guidelines coming from it are the sources of our calling.

The call is all of the above, depending on how you want to look at it, and which disciplines speak most powerfully for you. But even with these explanations and the many more that are possible, something mysterious and unexplained is at work when we hear calls in our lives. And that is just fine with most of us—we accept the experience of being called without having to know exactly why it happens. Most likely, upon examination, it happens for a variety of reasons. In my own experience, I have attributed the sense of a fairly constant calling to all four of the sources: theological, psychological, biological, and sociological. Depending on my thinking at the time, one or two may be more dominant than the others.

I appreciate both the science side of the call—there is no doubt that hormones and neurotransmitters have a role—and the spiritual or poetic side of being called to dedicate significant parts of our lives in ways we can't fully explain.

When I use the language of answering the call, truths are discussed in ways that those of us who are comfortable with poetry and metaphor and spiritual language will have a feeling for. There is an element of mystery involved in having a calling. We can't point to it like a coffee cup. So it belongs in the realm of human truth not dependent on science.

How to Read This Book

The eight chapters of this book are grouped into three parts that represent a logical sequence for answering your call, building as you proceed. The first section of the book discusses the most basic questions for answering your call; the later sections take on important refinements and action steps once you are on your way.

Each chapter begins with questions that we all have about answering our calls. The questions pose the problems and challenges we face, either in hearing the calls as they make themselves known or in responding to the calls once we hear them.

Part 1, "Getting Started with a Calling," contains the first three chapters, which clarify the concepts and get us moving in a positive direction for making our calls real.

Chapter 1, "What Is a Call?" defines what calls are and describes how they function. It also covers how we respond to calls, if we want to, and what kind of time dimension is at work when our busy lives are too crammed with activity to sense the calls we encounter.

Chapter 2, "Common Calls," provides guidance on the most common calls at work in people's lives and how to recognize them. Some calls are quite intellectual, whereas others come more from the heart. This chapter looks at how to think about calls so we can respond with intelligence, putting our natural talents to work at the life tasks we have already assumed.

Chapter 3, "Mightily Believe You Have a Calling," covers the most fundamental aspect of a called life: the belief that you have one. It starts with the question, How do I sense my calling in a world that does not help me discover it? The shallowness of the world causes considerable doubt and confusion for those who wish to heed their calls. This chapter provides one guarantee: it is absolutely certain that you will never answer your call if you don't mightily believe, in spite of all the evidence to the contrary, that you have one to begin with.

Part II, "Breathing Depth into Common Calls," begins with the biggest challenge to the calling process: sabotage in its many forms. It then moves on to forms of support for a calling, even the most demanding call of all, that of the provocateurs.

Chapter 4, "Endure the Saboteurs," describes a basic experience for persons who dare to act on their calling. Once you mightily believe in your calling, you will attract naysayers and negative people who want you to give up your calling because, in their opinion, you don't have what it takes to answer it and it is so silly in the first place. This chapter, using stories from literature and real life, explores how the negative ones work, how we invite them into our lives, and how to endure them and even grow because of them.

Chapter 5, "Pass On the Evocateur's Gift," discusses the nature of the support we receive from those who affirm our calling. The chapter looks at and describes this fundamental form of support in the process of being called. The challenge is, of course, that once you begin a called life for yourself, you are bound to help others on their quest.

Chapter 6, "Provoke the Stifling," explores a difficult life call that most of us will have to respond to during some periods and episodes in our lives. To accept a provocateur's calling we need special clarity and support and humor, lest we take the call too seriously. This chapter uses an historical example.

Part III, "Keeping Focus for the Long Term," does just that. This final section of the book contains two important chapters on how to do righteous battle with the ego and keep the deeper causes of life in mind as we go on throughout the decades.

Chapter 7, "Go Gently Against the Ego," examines the challenges of false messages and self-deception that can derail anyone on a mission. It provides principles, models, tips, and stories on how to go about addressing those challenges.

Chapter 8, "Work the Veil," concludes the book with insights offered from the people I interviewed. They had many thoughts to share. It prevails upon all wanting to live from a set and sequence of callings to learn that the veil between what is real and what is possible is indeed a thin one.

There are ample stories and quotes in the book to make the theory and models real and concrete. The stories come from people I know, those I interviewed, my own life, history, and literature.[3] They are meant to activate your imagination so you can think about stories and applications of your own.

You will also find questions and application exercises at the end of the chapters, again to support and challenge you as you muster up your will and energy, discernment and self-knowledge to answer your call. The book is designed to be informing, inspiring, and practical. I distinctly hope it is so. You can make it very practical by using the questions at the end of the chapters to think through your life and your decisions.

No one person will encounter all of the challenges described in this book, but most people will encounter many, along with others not mentioned.

Pursuing a life purpose has its periods of ease and grace, interspersed with difficulties, challenges, and hard work. Mentors and coaches, ideas and support from others, and most importantly, your own best thinking and highest intention can keep the journey from becoming a grind or an impossibility. You can fill your journey with meaning, embrace the chores that come with a calling, and with some good fortune and discipline, experience considerable joy.

Getting Started with a Calling

Since a called life is never a finished product, in significant ways we are always at the beginning and renewing stages of answering our calls. In this first part of the book we start with basic notions: what calls are and do (chapter 1), how we can recognize the types of calls that creep or crash into our lives (chapter 2), and how calls don't show up in our lives if we let the world, rather than our will, guide our decisions (chapter 3).

When I talk about basic notions I mean fundamental and foundational, not simple or remedial. There is nothing remedial about answering calls. It is all graduate-level work.

If you understand calls, recognize them when they show up, and believe you have received one or many over the course of your lifetime—especially when it doesn't feel like it—you will set the foundation for a called life.

What Is a Call? ①

THINK OF THE WORLD YOU CARRY WITHIN YOU. . . .
BE ATTENTIVE TO THAT WHICH RISES UP IN YOU AND SET
IT ABOVE EVERYTHING THAT YOU OBSERVE ABOUT YOU.
WHAT GOES ON IN YOUR INNERMOST BEING IS WORTHY OF YOUR
WHOLE LOVE; YOU MUST SOMEHOW KEEP WORKING AT IT.

Rainer Maria Rilke
Letters to a Young Poet

CALLS CREATE SPECIFIC and lasting effects, and they reveal themselves in many different ways. Before we explore their consequences or revelations, however, let's put the first question first: What is a call?

If we can address this question well we will have a beginning. The other questions asked in this opening chapter also belong near the beginning:

- What do calls do?
- What does it mean to respond to a call?
- When do calls happen?

Working Definitions

Calls are invitations from life to serve, to activate your will toward a cause worthy of you and the human family. They are purposes with a voice, visions turned into inner commands. Calls draw you into the specifics of a purpose and a vision.

A call is the impulse to move ahead in a meaningful way. It is a mind-body push into the future.

A call is passion, desire, and choice, all rolled into one.

A call is part intellectual and part emotional; your human will, moving you in one direction and not in a thousand other possible ones.

A call is sometimes heard as an inner voice, sometimes seen as an image or mental picture, sometimes felt as a self-administered kick in the butt. It urges you to go past the surface level and do something that has lasting value. It may be the message to stop working on the significant efforts that you are helping others with and instead to work on the significant efforts that are more uniquely yours.

Calls are the source of the lasting creativity in our lives.

Does this answer the question of what a call is? Of course not.

No one knows for sure what calls are. That is the best part about them. Calls remain in the realm of the mysterious. The experience of calls—or callings, or vocations, as some refer to them—has attracted its share of efforts at definition, including by me. (Vocations tend to be viewed as lifelong, career-type efforts. We'll use "call" more broadly than "vocation," but won't avoid the term.) If you know of anyone who has a precise or scientific definition, or a poetic or religious one, and you like it, use it. But don't pretend you know completely what a call is, any more than you can summarize what love is. It is useful with mysterious, complex life phenomena like calls not to confine the discussion to what they are, but also to ask what they do.

And calls do many things.

They provide soul-mandates, orders to live the large part of our lives, to attach ourselves to a cause that pulls us out of the limits of our personal history.

Calls command that you attach yourself to something infinite and lasting so you can escape the life you thought you deserved and replace it with the life you were meant for.

Calls create dissatisfaction with the successes in life that our egos wish so much to attain: money, security, status, even the little pleasures beautiful in themselves and banal when inflated to the level of reasons for living.

Calls pull us out of the psychic wounds and inhibitors we inherited. The wounds and limits come from parents who lovingly raised us for the most part, but messed up doing their best, and from the culture that negated the whole of us and instead made us partial people who would fit its purposes.

Calls create the urge to do something significant, providing the inner drive that informs us it is time to get on with it. They provide the sense of being drawn to contribute, to use our wisdom and gifts in ways that benefit others, that enhance life.

Calls draw us to the depth level of whatever roles we may already have. They turn insurance policy peddlers into advisers of needed financial security, grocery store employees into health and nutrition suppliers, doctors into healers, secretaries into stewards, businesspeople into entrepreneurs, bureaucrats into civil servants, writers into dream weavers, parents into co-creators of life.

With all these positive effects, you might think that people would spend the great bulk of their lives trying to respond to their calls. But most of us don't.

There are two significant reasons why we don't respond passionately and constantly to our calls. First, we don't always know how to do so; even when we know that calls exist and what they do we are a long way from having the wisdom to live them well. Second, we focus on other concerns and ignore or sidestep the depth level of our lives. We get distracted from the deep work and play out our lives on their surface, with considerable encouragement from our culture for diversion and avoidance.

For all the importance of calls, it is not often easy to figure out how to live in accordance with them. The process of staying aligned with a call can be a strenuous, even exhausting, struggle. The times in our lives when we are obviously in harmony with our call and flowing with it grandly are matched by times of dissonance, feeling out of sync, and grinding it out.

RESPONDING TO THE CALL

So what is answering a call all about?

As before, mystery takes over here, but it is worth attempting to explain, again as much by describing what a response requires of us as by what it is.

Answering your call is declaring yes to the invitation to live from your essence over and over again.

Answering a call is rising out of bed in the morning one more day to get the kids off to school, to go to the workplace, and to attend to the multiple stations in our lives so we can bring whatever it is we believe in into the world.

Answering a call takes refinement and discernment. Starting the response with "I want to do good" is a help, but not much of one. As Lily Tomlin says in her one-woman play *The Search for Intelligent Life in the Universe:* "When I was young I always wanted to be somebody. Now I know I should have been more specific."[1]

The specifics of how to answer a call show up in the themes of our lives and the energy we expend on them. For example, caring relationships. The community. Achievement and excellence. Spiritual growth. Service to those in need.

It also shows up in the roles we choose: Executive. Teacher. Parent. Board member. Craftsman. Artist.

When the roles support the life themes, we are in great shape and on the way to answering our calling. When they don't, we have some work to do.

Creating this alignment between what you are called to do and what you are really doing is crucial to the work of responding to calls. Like a colleague of mine, you may need to transform your work. This friend has a degree in dentistry. Not long ago, he ended a successful twenty-year career to move on to new work. He now devotes most of his time to working for his neighborhood association. If he had stayed with dentistry any longer, by his accounting, he was not going to be true to himself.

But the alignment we need to make may not be about change on the outside of our lives. It may be more about change on the inside. Most of this book is about the inner work of responding to the calls we find or the ones that find us.

Answering a call takes persistence, discipline, and stamina. After the initial yes, we answer the call by creating sets and subsets of long-term and short-term strategies, goals, and tactics.

The goals aren't the calling itself, however; they are only a best guess about what to get done to respond to the calling. Each goal takes more yeses, more affirmations and acts of will as we persist in our response to the calls we sense. And when working toward a goal stops working—and it often does—we have to open up our minds and hearts and listen again. Persistence needs its polar opposite: openness and willingness to stop the current plan and go in a new direction.

Responding to a call is easier at some times in a person's life than at others, but no matter how successful one particular stage, responding is never in lockstep to a set of instructions that show up in an email from God@aol.com.

Steve Sheppard is the CEO of Foldcraft, a member-owned furniture maker in southern Minnesota with 250 employees—or members, as they call themselves. It is a company that has been creating a strong culture of empowered and enlivened workers for over three decades, a social experiment of the highest order where free enterprise, callings, and adding value in the world go hand in hand.

With the success of Foldcraft, however—and it's being featured as exemplary by many—Steve still has questions about his response:

There are times when I feel I have not answered the call very well. I still feel responsibility for making people feel happy at work, although intellectually I know that I cannot achieve this. I hurt when someone leaves our organization under unpleasant circumstances. Or when our organization isn't as responsive to a new initiative or idea as I anticipated. . . .

I question the propriety of this "call" [to be CEO of the company] constantly.

Calls are neither constantly clear nor easy once we heed them.

The Danish philosopher Kierkegaard said that "we all come to life with sealed orders"—an apt metaphor for the internal searches we conduct just trying to find the envelope for different chapters of our lives.[2] You know you left it somewhere: In the rolltop desk, in the back panel of my briefcase maybe. It could be stuck with the family photos I never have time to put in the albums. I don't know where it is, but I swear I saw it once. It's gotta be here somewhere!

There are stories, of course—and you may know some personally— of people who have had a clear sense of a calling since their youth. Their focused response is to pursue a dream, and rising above or with circumstances, they achieve notable success by making the dream happen.

This book, however, is not primarily about such people. It is more about the many of us who don't have extraordinary minds or talents that point us in one obvious direction, who don't make the headlines with our stellar accomplishments or ever know what it is like to achieve the notable results of the gifted. Although our calls and responses to them are sometimes clear, they are often found way back in Kierkegaard's envelope.

Still, living a called life is not all mystery and drudgery by any means. Responding to a call can be a relief after a long search and considerable confusion. It can often feel joyous.

David Quammen, ecologist, essayist, and author of many books, including *The Song of the Dodo,* the beautiful, compelling scientific and historical look at the loss of species on the planet, sent me an email when I asked about his calling.[3] (He was also a high school buddy and a college friend who has become one of my life anchors, in great part because he has lived his passion. He does have an extraordinary mind, by the way, but I said the book would be *mostly* for those of us with a little less horsepower.)

Here is what Dave said about being called to writing:

Some writers, so they say, loathe writing but love having written. *What they mean is, it's bloody hard scary work. It is. However, I love it. Love it love it. When I'm spending a week doing research, reading journal papers, reviewing notes, making phone calls, I'm interested in the effort . . . but well, I get tired, nod off, wonder whether it's time yet to stop for lunch. When I'm actually* engaged *in the writing of an essay, a feature, or a book, however . . . the time flies by. I sit down at the computer with a cup of coffee at 8 A.M., blink once, become mesmerized, blink again, and it's 6 P.M., the coffee is half-drunk, my shirt is drenched with sweat, and maybe, maybe, I have three pages of workable, fixable first draft. This is ecstasy. This is life.*

As Dave illustrates as only a writer could, the work of responding to a call can be ecstatic, even around and through the parts of life, like research, that take considerable hunkering down.

If calls can be clarifying, they can also be terrifying. Calls take you beyond the confines of what you thought you knew to regions of high risk and the unknown.

I live in Kansas City, where no long-term resident can escape the lore about Harry Truman, nor would anyone want to. Truman's life was filled with great examples of feeling a call. When asked in his retirement which political job he had wanted the most, he answered simply: none. He had never wanted any of the jobs he had ended up serving in, including the most daunting of them all, President. Imagine Truman's fear in 1945 when FDR died a few months into his presidency, during which time the two had spent a total of ninety minutes together. Not exactly a great preparation for the momentous decisions ahead.

Truman often said that there were many others more qualified than he to do the job of the presidency. "But it is my job to do and I am going to do it," he would say, with a sense of the inevitability of a call.

From twentieth-century literature and J.R.R. Tolkien we observe another supreme example of responding to a call: when Frodo, with no credentials, the never-been-out-of-the-neighborhood regular-guy hobbit from the outskirts of Middle Earth, decides to bear the ring he has innocently inherited on the jaunting journey to its destruction. Surrounded by other creatures with more skill and intelligence and knowledge of the world, he sees the task fall to him and he claims it.

Like Harry Truman and the hobbit Frodo, we are sometimes burdened with the tasks set before us, called to work we would not have chosen.

I know a man closely related to my daughter-in-law—we'll call him Carl—who was looking forward to the recreation-filled days of retirement in his later fifties after years of flying around the world in his job as scientist for a global manufacturing firm. Then, shortly after he retired, his ever-active wife, Clare, came down with a strange disease that affected her like an intense stroke, and she lost some of her speaking skills and mobility. Carl inherited a new job, a tiring one of almost constant care and vigilance. As a devoted husband, he was called to serve his wife, and he did so, allowing the two of them to continue to enjoy long trips in their mobile home and their life as retirees and grandparents of six.

No one near him has heard a word of complaint from Carl.

Kierkegaard had a phrase for the soul-dread we experience when the calls we'd rather not face become crystal clear. He described responding to these calls as an encounter with "fear and trembling," a phrase for which he is well-known in philosophical circles. If we say yes in response to these calls we overcome the fear and trembling, or at least we get used to them.

From joy to dread, responding to calls provides a large sweep of feelings and reactions.

Not responding to calls also brings feelings and consequences, like boredom and anxiety. We can run from our calls and not respond to them, but I recommend you not waste your precious life in call-avoidance. You'll have to find another book to help you avoid your calls, or better yet, just turn on the television or consume for as long as you can stand it.

The all-time classic on avoiding calls is a poem that conjures up the anxiety and persistent dread that accompany doing so. It comes from Francis Thompson, the nineteenth-century British poet, whose "Hound of Heaven" personifies the call not just with a voice but with feet of persistent, steady pursuit.[4]

I fled Him, down the nights and down the days;
I fled Him, down the arches of the years;
I fled Him down the labyrinthine ways
Of my own mind; and in the mist of tears
I hid from Him, and under running laughter.
    Up vistaed hopes I sped;
    And shot, precipitated,
Adown Titanic glooms of chasmed fears,
From those strong Feet that followed, followed after.
    But with unhurrying chase,
    And unperturbed pace,
Deliberate speed, majestic instancy,
    They beat—and a Voice beat
    More instant than the Feet—
"All things betray thee, who betrayest Me."

Thus Thompson warns us not to betray our calls lest we pursue a life of futile fleeing, empty laughter, and hopes that turn to gloom.

Responding to a call is a choice that leaves you no choice. As with all mysteries of life, we are in a paradox here. Responding to your call means accepting the burden that sets you free. Calls have a way of choosing you, as they did Frodo and Harry Truman. We can say yes or delay the answer as long as possible, but we begin to live more fully when we answer in the affirmative, even if we don't understand what is going on.

Not to listen to your call is a self-inflicted spiritual crime of omission. Not to allow others to act on theirs is a victim-inflicted spiritual crime of commission.

Calls are serious business. Responding to them is how we make something worthwhile out of our lives.

Calls and the Times of Our Lives

The Greeks made a distinction between two kinds of time. Ordinary cook-the-meal, drive-to-work, review-the-email time they deemed *chronos* (hence, *chronological*). Meaning-steeped, whack-on-the-side-of-the-head, "Wow, this-is-awesome" time, they called *kairos*—a time for the spirit, making it a timeless time.

When the world experiences kairotic time our culture acquires mythic moments, symbolic dimensions in our collective psyche that structure the way we think about ourselves and the world. The year 1776 was a historical one chronologically, but from a kairotic point of view it was the beginning of democracy in the United States and the world. The moment when Neil Armstrong set foot on the moon in 1969 created space-age, planetary humanity on the blue marble spinning in the universe. These moments of kairos develop the symbols that take a permanent place in our consciousness and embody new sets of ideas, icons, and identity.

At the personal level, kairotic time often happens in predictable places: births, weddings, graduations—all the sizeable life passages we experience. But depth-time is more often unpredictable, and any and all moments when life's eternal energy pours into the ordinary events of our lives are spirit-loaded, timeless time. I remember the first time I saw a gray dolphin darting under the bow of our little catamaran beneath the glistening ocean surface in Florida—for a few seconds time stopped, and we were one with the forces of life.

Many parts of us live in chronological time. But the self, the deep inner guide, lives in kairotic time. Callings come from the kairotic dimension, popping through life in occasionally predictable but often surprising ways at unforeseeable moments. The chronology of our lives spin out from our decisions and make up the years, but our callings hit us at unexpected moments when our depths need to voice a new direction or outline another possibility not seen in the routine of the daily chronology.

Because calls come to us from this different time, we need to be quiet enough long enough often enough to heed them. This is why the literature on calls spells out the need to be quiet and listen. Being constantly busy with the chronos of daily duties gives us no time to sense the charged dimension of time that surrounds us.

When you feel you have to take a new direction in your work, when you feel the gentle nudge from your gut to pick up the phone and reconnect with an old friend, when you decide to give up an old hobby so you can be more in touch with your kids—these are how the soul-urgings of calls make themselves known. The mind may flood with an image, the chest may heave in disgust at the thought of doing something one more time, a dream may bring its message in clear or murky symbols, a prayer may provide an answer to a tough question.

Kairotic time percolates or blasts, seeps or explodes into the chronology of our lives whenever it does—and we find ourselves being called.

The Nature of Calls

Calls may be mysterious, but we can learn what they are and what impact they have by observing our actions, our thoughts, and the reasons we feel compelled to serve in some way.

In our nature at a deep and abiding level there is the drive to do the things that matter, and at the same time, not always to know how, and to avoid the work that calls point to for us all.

Our responses to the calls we discern can be difficult and take much effort both to design and to execute. Our responses to calls constitute the essence of our lives as we move ahead on a path of meaning that only we can choose. Whether clarifying or terrifying, responding to a call is freely accepting the duty we sense to will lasting value into the situations we encounter. Confronting the fear of accepting a call is the best way to move into the joys that a call brings.

Calls break through the routines of time and bequeath us spirit-laced time, rich in the soul dimensions that only they can bring to the everyday roles we choose and the ordinary chapters of living a life.

In the next chapter, we look at the most common calls and provide some methods for reviewing the calls you may encounter in your everyday existence.

EXERCISE: THINKING ABOUT THE NATURE OF CALLS

- How do your calls show up: as feelings, images, thoughts, voices?
- Do you have any models for those living a called life in your family or close friends? If not, can you find some? How? If so, what about calls did you learn from these people?
- Do any of your current roles naturally lend themselves to a sense of calling? Which ones?
- When have you felt the power of kairos break through your ordinary awareness? Is there any pattern to these times?
- Are you avoiding a call currently and is it making you miserable, like the Hound of Heaven? Have you ever avoided a call in the past?

Common Calls (2)

WE HAVE DESCRIBED CALLS and our response to them. Now, let's be very practical and look at how calls work in our everyday lives.

Mother Teresa often talked about her calling to work with the poor. Before a meaning-filled train journey she had been a teacher; after she had a prayerful conversation with God on that trip, she changed her life mission and served the poor. Her life was one of the great modern examples of answering a call.

But for two reasons, in this book we will concentrate less on the inspiring examples like Mother Teresa, although we won't ignore them. First, her life was very different from the lives of most of us who have normal family and work roles, kids or grandkids or aging parents, jobs we want to build into careers, and careers we want to be fulfilling. On top of that we have life maintenance chores—we buy groceries and make mortgage payments, cut the grass and clean the refrigerator. Mother Teresa, a shining portrait of a called life devoted to service, most likely had a lot of normal life activities too, but she is hard to relate to. Her life is saintly in the extreme.

Second, Mother Teresa had a conversation with God in a prayerful moment that marked the rest of her life. My experience is that most of us have multiple conversations and calling moments in a lifetime, and often we have to move on when the calling is anything but clear and singular.

So the questions we address in this chapter are these:

- If you have talent but not overwhelming gifts, how can you shape your response to callings so that you give meaning to your daily activity?
- Can you consider the various calls in any systematic way as you respond to the many sides of life, all of which are worth living with high intention?
- How can you use your past, review the calls you excelled in answering, the ones you managed well enough, and the ones you botched up terribly, so you can move into the future with greater wisdom?

CALLS BOTH OBVIOUS AND SUBTLE

There are those among us who have a talent and an aptitude so well developed and seemingly such a gift of genetic endowment and upbringing that their answer to their call is to develop that talent or that aptitude to its fullest. By doing so, they endow all of us. Musician, athlete, and entrepreneur are a few of the roles that seem to invite the supertalented and that are brought to us by the media.

Tiger Woods is a cultural athletic endowment. Ravi Shankar is a musical one. Einstein, a scientific one. And there are thousands like them. It is a pity when we observe someone with great talent who does not pursue it for whatever reason. We say that is a waste and wonder why it happened, sometimes finding answers and sometimes not.

But these standouts, for a different reason than Mother Teresa, are not unlike her; they are equally difficult for all of us of more average talent to relate to.

Most people are not given an extraordinary talent to develop, nor, as much as they may reflect, a clear direction during a train trip while in prayer. What happens in the everyday world is that we discover our talents and our flaws, come across problems that intrigue us and roles that absorb us, and make commitments to give our best. Some of the roles we take on last for decades, if not a lifetime. Some last for a much shorter time.

In the stew of everyday problems and ordinary life tasks we gain opportunities to do something about them. This, combined with the cultivation of our talents as we discover them, helps us arrive at our callings. We find ourselves summoned to make something better, to do something worthwhile. When we say yes to the summons, we are acting on our calls.

These are the less obvious calls that engage our minds and hearts, do not win us trophies, and yet make all the difference to society and to ourselves when we make the decision to do something worthwhile. People who answer these calls include the schoolteacher devoted to sparking the minds of his students. The sales manager wanting to deliver a superior service and develop her people to the fullest. The engineer designing the best, safest, most efficient building. The parents patiently doing homework with their child. The social worker addressing one more difficult case.

Unlike the mega-calls for the supertalented or saintly, a portfolio of everyday callings is at work for us at any particular time in our lives. One or two calls may take up most of our time—such as being a good parent and adding as much value as possible through our daily work—but other smaller calls—like staying true to a friend facing cancer and needing support—may also work their way into our lives. It is the waxing and waning of calls during the months and years, duties and roles that need our best intentions and solid attention, that create a life. Most of us live a portfolio of calls of our own making.

To describe this kind of approach to multiple calls, there is a quote on a grave at Arlington National Cemetery that says it well:

> Few of us have the greatness to bend history itself. But all of us have the opportunity to change a small portion of events. It is from numberless acts of courage and belief that human history is shaped.

Having courage and belief in the numberless tasks and routines of living a life is answering a call. The quote is from Robert Kennedy.

This portfolio idea needs some emphasis. Some of those who support the notion of callings get entirely too grandiose about it. I once heard a speaker at a convention talking about destiny and calls and using Jesus and Martin Luther King as examples for the audience. Although I found the stories inspiring and sensed the speaker's intent, I think he had the emphasis wrong.

I wanted to tell him to chill out, to get considerably less heroic about it all. We are called to live courageously in the little events more often than the historically significant ones. Some calls are obvious and big; most are subtle and small. Look for and live the small ones.

Being a mother, a great mother who raises loving whole kids, is a calling.

Being a ditchdigger may be a calling too.

Years ago, while I was giving a seminar, a man I will call Romanelli (not his real name; I can only remember the Italian part) told me a story about his grandfather, who was a laborer in his son's (Romanelli's father's) construction firm of the same name. The son had gotten the education, and now it was the grandson's turn to work in the family business, starting with the physical labor part of it, and learn from the bottom up.

One hot summer day, the grandson was digging ditches and going through the motions halfheartedly. Grandfather Romanelli was watching and decided it was time to teach his heir a little about callings.

In his heavily accented English, which you can add with your imagination, the older man approached the teenager. "Why are you not digging with energy, boy?" queried the elder. "We gotta long a way to go down this road."

"Grandpa," answered the grandson, "you know this is lousy work and I can't wait until it's over."

"When you diggin' the ditch," said Grandpa with teachable-moment emphasis and strength in his voice, "you dig the ditch with pride. That's no ordinary ditch. That's a Romanelli ditch!"

We assume ordinary roles. We can make them more than ordinary when we will them to a higher level.

The Working Quadrant of Calls

There are many such calls to significance in ordinary life. In this section I describe the quite common ones, and I use a simple two-axis grid to categorize them. When I hear people describe what it is that they are trying to accomplish in their lives, how they are adding value, and what their inner voice is urging them to address, I hear the following calls more than others. I encourage you to add your own to the list, because this is not intended to be comprehensive, and make your own grid, because the categories are also open to additions.

It doesn't take much observation to see that calls come in polar opposites. Where one person feels attracted to a field exploring an inner frontier, like psychotherapy, another will be attracted to an outer frontier, like cataloguing the world's tectonic plates. It's a yin-yang phenomenon. What one person is drawn to and develops his gifts for, another abhors.

As Ecclesiastes reminds us: there is a time for every purpose (and call) under heaven.

The horizontal axis of the grid shows the internal and external polar opposites of calls. In a field such as science, for example, there is a spectrum from internal, which stays primarily in a mental mode or abstract state, to external, the more visible one. The internally driven scientist works in primary research and knowledge for its own sake; the externally driven scientist applies science to the world and builds or makes things.

Those driven by calls to the internal focus on creating mental models and knowledge; those responding to calls to the external concentrate on applications and working models in the real world of space and time.

Imagination versus applied imagination. Knowledge versus applied knowledge.

For the vertical axis of the grid, I've chosen to make the spectrum the head and the heart, or the fields of human endeavor divided along our thoughts and our emotions. This leaves out the body for now, but we will have a word on that later. The head is obviously about cognition, and the heart concerns the emotional intelligence work that imbues calls of many kinds.

So here is the grid.

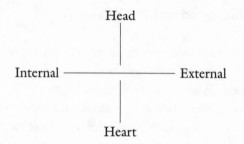

The danger in any such illustration is oversimplification. Of course, much human endeavor combines head and heart and is both internal and external. But I use the grid to describe the degree of internal-external and head-heart, not to isolate one calling as solely one type or another.

What's useful about making these distinctions is that in pursuing a call, you can match your strengths and analyze your history as a source of knowledge for the decisions ahead of you. You can better discern what your options are. It may be time, for instance, for someone who has worked in the field of human emotions and intelligence—customer service professionals, for example—to redirect themselves to the head spectrum of the field, to analyze customer contact patterns and devise new service options, perhaps. Same field, different spin on the calling.

There are an endless number of calls by virtue of our uniqueness. We sit firmly in the world of paradox here, as the career counselor giving the college student advice says: "Remember, you are unique, just like everybody else."

Like genus and species and subspecies, the list of calls could go into the thousands. But knowing the greater call patterns is the place to start. Then refine them to your own purposes and that of others.

When you support an adolescent beginning her quest, it is helpful to teach her to make the distinction between the joys and demands of the call of the family and those of the call of the marketplace. Later she can decide for herself if she wants to devote herself to the details and daily drama of raising kids in a Cleveland suburb, pursue equity financing to buy a bagel franchise, or both.

COMMON CALLS

Knowing how many calls exist is not as important as understanding how to respond to the real thing and how to combine them in harmonious ways to make a life of meaning. When we respond well, the choices we make create a beautiful life tapestry worthy of hanging in the Call Hall-of-Fame. When we respond poorly, we end up with an unsightly mess, not worthy of hanging anywhere.

Here are some of the most common calls and a description of where they could be placed on the matrix.

THE CALL TO FAMILY: EXTERNAL HEART

This is the most widely received of calls. We seem hardwired genetically to devote ourselves to the good of our families. One generation's care for the next, or the former, takes on the dimensions of a calling when we see that the well-being of those we are connected to as family depends in great part on the love, resources, and attention we provide.

THE CALL OF THE MARKETPLACE: EXTERNAL HEAD

This common call activates millions as they formulate plans to build the business in which they participate and make free enterprise the playground where they focus their talents. Their natural bent is to think about beating the competition, getting more customers, increasing shareholder value, and generating wealth. This call, like the others, can take a person out of balance if pursued to the exclusion of other calls.

THE CALL TO LEADERSHIP: EXTERNAL HEART AND HEAD

This call most often combines new ways of thinking with the ability to influence others. Authentic leadership shows up whenever someone facilitates and stimulates collective change for the good of the whole. The failure of stepping up to a call to leadership shows up in lack of vision, stamina, communication know-how, and most notably, courage. This call shows up in all walks of life, integrating unchanging purpose with continuous change, generating productive action stemming from core values.

THE CALL TO SCHOLARSHIP: INTERNAL HEAD

Far from the day-to-day hype of pop culture, those in the community of scholars are called to advance the knowledge of humankind through research and the rigors of their discipline. Those called in this way often work behind the scenes for the good of humankind.

THE CALL TO SPIRITUAL SERVICE: EXTERNAL HEART

This one is not reserved for the clergy, but activates anyone whose devotion to God or a higher source is strong in their lives. Clergy in any religion make this call the cornerstone of their lives. The examples we have of those living this type of call are huge—from all the saints and Mother Teresa to Aunt Millie, who never missed her daily prayers and never had anything but a kind word for everyone.

THE CALL TO A HIGHER MORAL ORDER AND JUSTICE: EXTERNAL HEART

This call accompanies many of the other calls and it is a powerful force in history as good tries to overcome the regressive forces in our nature. Sometimes a provocateur like Nelson Mandela emerges on the world stage to usher in a new moral order. In our everyday lives, this call may be lived by a community trying to make the best use of its economic resources for all, poor and not poor. The distinguishing feature of these calls is that they are ennobling in and of themselves and act as a cornerstone of free societies.

A rare and powerful form of this call is when someone endures a life wound to turn it into a passionate cause. A person is deeply injured by an injustice or a tragedy—a murder of a loved one, an environmental disaster that destroys a neighborhood. The victim, rather than healing the wound privately, transforms the inner pain and anger into an outer cause. The women who created Mothers Against Drunk Driving (MADD) are perhaps the most widely known example.

THE CALL OF THE ROUTINE:
INTERNAL HEAD OR HEART

The counterpoint to the call to a higher moral order and justice is this call to take on the insignificant-in-themselves tasks and routines and transform them into acts of human accomplishment. As long as we have bodies and live in space and time, large numbers of the human family will be serving food and cleaning buildings and processing claims and sorting mail, even if it's email. No higher moral order here, but it has to get done. People with this call commit themselves as evocateurs to breath life into the ordinary, to make the menial meaningful. Although the routines may be external, the work to infuse them with meaning is internal.

THE CALL OF THE PROFESSIONS:
MAINLY EXTERNAL HEAD AND HEART

(A word of explanation: the engineer is a typical head call; the social worker a call of the heart.)

Those who start out as engineers or chemists or nutrition specialists transform themselves when they get this call. They go from thinking about making a living through their profession to thinking about giving back to the world through the positive impact their profession can make. Those who respond to this career call are connected to the deeper aspects of their work. Whole professions occasionally get denigrated, like lawyers and car salespersons, so these people have special work to do.

THE COMMUNITY CALL: EXTERNAL HEART

The glue that holds together the quality of our lives in communities consists of the millions of people responding to the community call. These people are lured by the vision of enhancing the quality of life in their communities; they volunteer on boards, work in not-for-profit organizations. Taken to the limit, they are professional volunteers.

THE CALL OF NATURE: EXTERNAL AND HEAD OR HEART

Even among the ultra-urbanized who believe that bread comes from the shelf at the grocery store, magically concocted at a bakery somewhere, the call to nature continues to draw many of us to our biological or natural state. From visiting the national parks, to tending to the garden tomatoes, to working on local issues to preserve wetlands and wild habitats for distressed species, this call is a powerful one for many planetary citizens.

THE CALL TO BEAUTY: LOCATION DEPENDS ON THE ARTIST AND THE MEDIUM

(That is why I have placed it in the middle of the grid.)

This is where the artists hang out, whatever their medium. Those who hear this particular call have a need to create art for their brothers and sisters, to collect it, display it, or somehow feed their souls with regular and frequent visits to the deeper dimensions of life that great art and beauty take us to.

THE CALL TO PUBLIC SERVICE: LOCATION DEPENDS ON THE PUBLIC SERVANT AND THE PATH TAKEN

This is the call to serve in government. It includes calls and subcalls, from the military to elected positions to lifelong civil service in a variety of executive departments. Answering this call—which has been much denigrated by those campaigning against "the bureaucrats" over the past several decades—attracts many who want to make a difference in making our governing processes serve the greater whole.

Here is how these calls look on the grid. I have added a few others to be specific, like prayer, a spiritual call for those in convents and monasteries, and professions, like teaching and writing.

Internal		External	
Scholarship		Teaching	**Head**
Research		Applied research	
Writing		Marketplace	
		Profession	
	Beauty		
	Public service	Leadership	
		Nature	
Routine		Family and community	**Heart**
Prayer		Spiritual service	
Spiritual service		Moral order and justice	

External calls are more common than internal calls because most people are called to do something that is outwardly visible that takes an already-existing social form, like a profession. My observations and many conversations and interviews lead me to believe that at least 80 percent of us respond to external calls. On the head-to-heart scale, it is much closer to 50-50.

WHAT ABOUT THE BODY?

While head and heart both go into any athletic or dancing career, the body alone is a calling for a significant portion of the human race. You may add to the previous list of calls the calls to use the body. Craftspeople, masseurs, and all those who work with their hands to heal and create beauty and function and value are responding to such a call.

There is no question that some are called to perform with their body as the medium for their work. Eventually, when the body ages, many of those gifted in this way are called to evolve into another aspect of their work or another career entirely, so they can again be called to do something significant. Frequently the change is from performance to coaching or mentoring, from the external to the internal.

But not always.

Henry Moore, the sculptor, used his hands to create beauty into his nineties. When asked how he could continue this work for so many decades he said he had such a consuming passion for it that he could never chip it all away.

GIVING THE ROLE MUCH MORE THAN YOU THOUGHT YOU HAD

One word of caution.

Merely accepting or carrying out the duties of a role you like is not responding to a call. Using language like a "portfolio of common calls" can make it sound as if all life tasks are callings. In fact, a role only becomes a call when you will greatness and lasting spiritual substance into it, when you see the possibilities for something transcendent in a role that doesn't on the surface seem to have many lasting possibilities. Digging ditches or being a parent or working for the government is a role, a job, or a calling, depending on how much courage and intention you bring to it.

The role turns into a calling when something inside you feels summoned to live the essence of the role and when you say yes to the summons. When you provide ample amounts of care and intention to a role's root meaning and when you surrender to its most profound mystery, you transform the role into a calling.

When many of us talk about our marriages, or raising a family, or a job we have taken, or even a position on a board that we accepted, we often reflect on what our decisions got us into. "If I had known what this was going to take ahead of time, I never would have done it. What was I thinking?" shriek our egos out of a sense of being trapped and burdened.

Yet when we hang in there and keep saying yes, keep surrendering to the largeness of the task, when we negate our ego and its search for ease and a pain-free life, we start to transform our roles into callings. We live with the painful joy of knowing that we took on life with all we had.

Building a Portfolio of Calls

The obviously gifted have the challenge of using their gifts for the world's benefit, whereas the more moderately talented inherit the challenge of living with high purpose and intention in the ordinary roles that society provides.

Living with high intention in the roles we choose leads to the everyday great-ness that can come with a portfolio of calls over the decades that mark our lives. History calls a few to greatness, but life calls all of us to make a difference in the situations we choose and into which we are sometimes thrown.

Our talents and preferences may take us to thinking or feeling, or internal or external work, but opportunities to respond to life's duties more completely and humanly, if sometimes in hiding, are always near.

In the next chapter, we look at how the world around us would rather we stay chronologically bound to the surface of these roles than listen to the voice from kairotic time that can give roles soul depth. But we can believe our way past the shallow dimensions of the world if we insist that our calls make themselves known, and when they do, respond to them with clear and full intention.

EXERCISE: REVIEWING YOUR CALL HISTORY

Take some time, as much as you find valuable, and go back over the major chapters of your life to see what calls you were responding to that made up your life tasks at that time. Then evaluate your response to those calls—a simple assessment can help you see if you gave it your all but didn't have enough skill, or if you had the aptitude but not the desire.

Here are two examples of life chapters: early career in New York and child-rearing years in university community.

You can use the decades of your life as a handy way to divide it into chapters, even if the chapters don't fit precisely into ten-year increments. The following examples may help prompt your own thinking:

DOMINANT CALLS AT PLAY	MY RESPONSE AND EVALUATION
Early-career chapter, twenties	
Call of the marketplace	Overenthused and slightly delusional; far too many hours and ramped up expectations.
	About the only passion I had.
Forties chapter	
Call of the routine	Attended well to the everyday aspects of career and family.
Call of the family	Poured considerable passion into the extended family, especially my nieces and nephews.
Call of the profession	Made a halfhearted attempt to give back to the world through advancing the profession of civil service. Not very well done, Was going through the motions. Didn't like my job or boss very well.

Think about your life chapters and the calls you responded to, those you ignored, and those you heard faintly in the distance but didn't devote enough of yourself to respond in a meaningful way. Consider the calls that make up your life now and what new calls may make themselves heard as your life progresses.

Mightily Believe You Have a Calling   3

I HAVE CALLED YOU BY NAME AND YOU ARE MINE.

Isaiah

ALTHOUGH CALLS CAN and do show up in everyday life, the difficulties in answering them are many. Believing that you are experiencing a call in the first place is a big challenge—so fundamental in fact that we'll discuss it as our initial, most basic hurdle. The challenges to answering your calls we'll explore in this chapter concern their very existence, because so often your daily experience and the world you encounter is anything but call-conducive.

Here are the questions we want to address in this chapter:

- How can you persist with your sense of calling in a society that aims large amounts of its resources at keeping you shallow?
- How can you stay patient enough to live your calling during those chapters of your life when much of your activity doesn't shine with purpose?
- How can you live out the limitless possibilities of a called life when your life is creased and bound by limiting circumstances?

LISTENING PAST THE SOCIAL NOISE

The social messages that divert us from our calls begin innocently enough early in our lives, when we are learning how to operate morally in a world of people: "Share your toys, Johnny, or your friends won't think you are a very nice boy." As we mature, the same vehicles for these early messages—the voices of those in authority—may support us as we try to answer our true callings. Helpful suggestions from a teacher who provides new vision or a board that invites you to participate as a director can make big and positive impacts. These messages from the world as we encounter it can be invitations in the right direction for composing a called life.

But although help may come through the culture, let us not be fooled: the dominant social drummer pounds a commercial and conforming beat that is intense and relentless. Madison Avenue tells us what is hot—on the radio we listen to on the way to the grocery store, on the billboard messages we see on the way to work. During tonight's trek through Web land, the homepage will tell us what is going on that matters and what we should give our attention to. The beat of society's drum thumps rhythmically, constantly, both in the forefront and in the background of our lives, and when we aren't giving our conscious attention to social messages we let the drummer's pulses affect us on an unconscious level.

Paul Anderson, the Bay Area coach and consultant whom you met in the introduction, offers his experience of the influence of the social voice. "[Earlier in life] I responded to what now feel like false calls, though maybe I needed to go there first," he writes, looking back on his early life chapters. "The calls came from society, like majoring in economics and finance and spending quite a few years in related fields."

Much like people who live near airports and learn to block out airplane noise, we adapt to the social beat because it is the background sound we are used to. We all make our life choices while tapping our toes to the beat of the social drum and we are at best only partially aware that the choices we consider fall into the very narrow range of human possibility that our culture allows. Meanwhile, the beat continues to pound out its core message: *Don't think too hard, someone else has done the thinking for you. Sign on the dotted line and don't worry. Come, follow the beat.*

If your parents didn't convince you to marry someone of the same religion, your boss will tell you what you ought to do on your climb to the corner office as the vice president of overhead. These impostor calls coming straight from the culture take the benign-looking form of help from those in positions of authority. A grandmother warns her beloved thirteen-year-old granddaughter "to be sensible." Being sensible in this case means, "Don't follow your gifts into music; play it safe and get a professional degree." Well-meaning advice from families and others in authority diverts many from responding to their deeper calls.

When listened to without discernment, the social drummer pounds out confusion, turning even the helpful parts of the social voice into noise.

The cultural beat becomes a cacophony of pulsings and imperatives that drown out our inner voice's ability to find the way to our authentic work.

Although many caught in this shallow and confusing world look desperate and out of touch, many more carry on looking quite poised and together. They hold their confusion on the inside, wondering what they are about, why the rat race is so demanding, and whether they will have the stamina to keep on.

MAKING MONEY AND THE SOCIAL DRUMMER

One of the very powerful social beats concerns the view of money and work.

The overwhelming social message is to focus on acquiring money. We all know people who are driven to make more money no matter how much they have. After all, it's good for the economy to earn and spend healthily. It's patriotic to consume whatever we can.

The movie *Wall Street*—which may achieve Hollywood classic status but stands as a great period piece on the greed of the eighties at the very least—provides a striking portrayal of this obsession. The young hero, fresh out of school, starting a life and looking for role models, encounters an exciting character of obvious business success, the flamboyant Gordon Gekko, who lives life large. At first the youth thinks Gekko's energy and creativity may be a source of creative capitalism and self-expression. But by the middle of the movie he is confused, as he assesses whether Gekko's drive to make money is positive or destructive.

His confusion is understandable.

From the outside looking in, especially to the unpracticed eye, the drive for money in any profession could seem to be a true calling to pursue excellence. A healthy, excellence-driven professional and a sick, money-driven professional may look the same on the outside: they are both very busy people doing many of the same things, spending long hours out of intense commitment, and earning big salaries.

But what is happening on the inside of those people is vastly different. *Making money is only one measure, and an external one at that, of what is going on.* People who are answering their call find self-expression through their work, achieve excellence and raise standards, and meet real human needs. The money-driven souls are after the big reward alone, pursuing proof that by making lots of money they are happy or at least better off than those who don't have as much.

In *Wall Street*, in Hollywood nick-of-time fashion, the young hero finally decides that the money- and power-mad Gekko is a wounded, dangerous, lost soul, sickened by the social pathology and suffering from the curse of Midas. When he realizes the depth and perversity of Gekko's obsession, he yells at him in disgust: "How many yachts can you water-ski behind?"

One, most likely, but someone will always be there to sell Gekko another yacht, or to sell you or me another television—the one we really need.

GOING BENEATH THE NOISE

The first step, then, for all who have a desire to live a life of sustained purpose, is to ignore the social din whenever possible, whether it is about money or power or being cool. We can buy nice things and pursue careers and do the normal, and then we have to pursue the abnormal, go contrary to fashion, swim upstream. We need our own set of drums with which to beat our own rhythms.

You must mightily believe that beneath the noise is a call to a deeper life that only you can respond to in the unique ways that your gifts allow and your life path has led you.

This is a belief in a deeper message, an important purpose or set of purposes that keeps the soul on target in a world of consuming and conforming and norming to a social mean that saps passion and wastes time. This is a belief in an essential you.

MAINTAINING PURPOSE WHILE MANAGING THE DOLDRUMS

Among the unwelcome features of life are the large periods of time when we engage in activity that is not in itself bad or worthless but that just doesn't carry a big psychological punch. After the marriage begins, when the honeymoon is a memory captured in a picture book, the work of maintaining the marriage and the family starts. After the career is launched with all its promise, the work of staying focused for the long haul, managing the ups and downs over time, becomes the daily chore.

When the rush of the beginning stages is gone, when the motivational tapes no longer pack a punch, when you live long periods with little inspiration, in sum, when the wind is gone from your life's sails, you encounter the doldrums, one of life's primary call-negating periods.

Frederic Hudson and Pamela McClean of the Hudson Institute of Santa Barbara are superb teachers of what happens in the doldrums.

They taught me to spot them and explained how unprepared most of us are for these long stretches.

Living your call even in the midst of these flat and uninspiring times is a critical skill and mindset to develop. (Much of this book is devoted to describing what kind of thinking is needed to pull this off.) Although we can experience the doldrums in parenting and everything else we do, some thoughts about our work life can get us started on the discussion.

Our work starts with a job, for most of us, something that we are lucky enough to "find" or "get." The job is out there, and if we look hard enough we can discover it and gain the means to pay our bills. The point of control for this search—unless you are a natural entrepreneur or at the top of your class—is as much with those making the offer as with those making the search. That is why one "gets lucky to find" such a good job.

But in a normally healthy economy of job creation, it doesn't take too long for most to go beyond the job-holding phase to the career management phase. We know this shift occurs when the point of control moves from those making the offer to those who are searching.

Unlike the job seeker who says, "Where will I be lucky enough to find good work?" the question for those managing careers becomes, "Who is going to be lucky enough to have me come work for them?" or "What kind of business do I want to create?"

This shift in control—from the job market to the person with the career journey—makes discovering and living a calling more possible. The chore of keeping a job evolves into the drama of creating a career, and the self-actualizing features of career-crafting engage the mind and heart.

Still, almost all the careers I have observed or had the privilege to coach include the doldrums. The long haul of a work life is rarely spiked with perfectly timed adventure and growth and newness. Exciting careers have flat periods, months and years of doing some of the same things that become routine.

Wouldn't it be nice if the manager of someone in the career doldrums came to him and declared: "We have noticed that the travel is getting to you and that the trips to San Antonio and Houston are becoming a bit routine. So we have decided to cut back on those meetings for you, give you a few very exciting tasks, and throw in a few

European junkets every quarter, so you can stay fresh, OK? How does that sound?"

This declaration is from the It-Will-Never-Happen Department.

So although a career can have excitement, it is laced, sometimes even laden, with doldrums and routine, sameness and flat times.

Although a calling may begin with a job and continue with a career, it doesn't end in either place. A calling is a long-haul proposition with a daily commitment to renew and recommit. We go from jobs to careers if we are at all skillful and willful, but for the purposes of answering a call, a career is nowhere near enough.

To handle the doldrums, we need to go with our core longing.
We need to will ourselves past career management into deeper territory.
Callings start where careers leave off.

To experience a calling, a seeker has to delve under the surface of a career of busyness or sameness and find significance and a sense of lasting contribution. Such work demands developing a higher form of will. It takes a mindset and a heartset that is beyond the norm.

Nearly two decades into a corporate career, most of it as a consultant, this well-known consultant and author had a conversation that took him past the doldrums. Peter Block described it to me this way:

The work came closer to a calling about twenty-five years later [out of college]. I was in Stockholm at a conference. I was there to run a small workshop and out of curiosity I attended a talk by a philosophy professor, Peter Koestenbaum. He talked of every person's need to confront the questions of destiny, isolation, meaning, death, relationship, and spirituality. The seriousness with which he spoke knocked me over. I had heard the words but never thought they were every person's concerns. After that talk, I went to see him and asked him if he would work with me as a client. As he worked with me, I began to accept, in my fortieth year, that something more was to be pursued in my life.

Block was spurred on to his vocation, past the success of his booming career in the training and organizational learning field, one in which he had already created his first best-selling book. He believed he had something bigger to address.

Still, the doldrums don't permanently disappear because of one-time conversations. The encounter with his mentor Peter Koestenbaum was the start of a different drumbeat for Peter Block, but hardly the end of the old one. The journey from head-engaging careers built around our egos to heart-reverberating vocations founded in our souls is usually a long one, and some of it travels over very stale and stagnant water. The doldrums appear any time the routine of the days and weeks and months starts to take the shine off the significance of the moment.

Career people with the ability to seize the magic in the moment and make their work a vocation, who expand their work into a calling that elevates the spirits of those whom they contact, are our models. The regular magic-making of people answering their call can happen only when they have beliefs, mighty beliefs. Mightily believing, in spite of all the facts to the contrary, is what breaks the bounds of ordinariness and set us on our way to significance.

One secret for keeping your calling alive is to declare the direct opposite of your doldrums experience. You negate the negation of your call and deem it something else.

When your career stalls in work that feels separated from meaning, precisely at this time you must affirm your work purpose, you must declare that the calls will come.

Override the feeling of staleness with an energizing and totally opposite thought. Doing so is an act that wills purpose into the seemingly purposeless. It is an absurd act of faith and defiance that defends your core being from the absurdity of the meaningless parts of the world and your life.

*"Making one more sales call is a way to provide service, needed and nec-
essary and humanizing service, to the customers in my marketplace."*
*"Handling this angry customer is not my favorite thing all the time, but
if I can help him go from frustration to a better mood, I have done
a little good."*
*"Going over these numbers is a pain in the rear, but it is a part of my
providing stewardship for this organization."*
*"I may be a programmer (or customer rep or consultant) like many
others, but I have something of lasting value to add here."*

Maintaining a sense of purpose, then, reminding yourself of the lasting value of your work, even the more mundane features of it, is one of
the essential tasks to sustain a call, and turn a career, or even a job, into
a vocation that elevates humanity.

THE MONASTERY VERSUS THE DOLDRUMS

In this lesson of making magic through the doldrums, monks have
much to teach. Monks take vows to stay in one monastery the whole of
their lives, to do ordinary work. They are spiritual specialists answering
a call to live in the antidramatic confines of monastic life. They choose
to live a life of significant insignificance. Confronting the mundane is a
huge part of their spiritual discipline, willing and praying meaning into
it. And waiting, of course, waiting to see what illumination may come
with the patience to do only the simple, only the unspectacular.

Author Michael Downey puts it this way: "In the ache of the ordinary,
the monk's mind may wander, and he may wonder: Will there ever be just
one Friday when it's not tomato soup and cheese sandwiches for supper?
What is the point of this life? Why don't I do something?"[1]

So monks plunge into the routine for a lifetime, to see what is really
there. And they stick with it, making no effort to escape the conditions
of sameness that create doldrums for most of us. They know that doldrums are more a state of mind and heart, a lack of commitment and
mindset, than an external condition.

Monks know that every day is a day with limitless possibilities. As monastic expert Downey put it: "We need to stand still long enough, stay in one place awhile, sink roots deep enough to see the sacred in (an ordinary) Wednesday."[2]

Monks mightily believe they have a calling. From them we can learn. Anyone who wants to answer the call of family or the professions through the inevitable doldrums can take inspiration from the monks.

Taking the Execs to the Monastery

One of my firm's leadership programs ends with a four-day trip to Aspen, during which time we discuss ethics, soak up the atmosphere of the great thinkers and of the Aspen Institute, and engage the big questions of human nature, corporate social responsibility, and our capacity for good and evil. In the previous five months, we have spent days with the business leaders in more mundane places like hotel conference rooms, studying more earthly topics like strategy and finance, and working on emotional intelligence skills for executives.

But Aspen caps it off. And on the second to the last day we head to Snowmass to the monastery to meet Fr. Theophane, and Fr. William and Brother Micah. We discuss contemporary issues and we attend one of their services and join them with some Gregorian chant. And they share their monastic commitments and doubts. The monks talk about their callings.

We take pictures and buy books and gifts at their bookstore. And we drive back to Aspen moved by their authenticity, courage, and depth of their inner lives.

On this last day of the intense five-month experience, the executives consider what they are being called to do in the next phases of their work and family and community life. They have seen the radical callings of the robed and prayerful monks. They use the monastery experience to reflect on their own calling, and the necessary commitment to living a life of meaning.

FOCUSING ON THE LIMITLESS WITHIN YOUR LIMITING CONDITIONS

Mightily believing in a calling despite the social noise and even during the doldrums are two problems to manage in living your call. A third is that the calling, and the expansiveness it evokes, needs to be lived out in the confines of totally ordinary duties and roles that are often anything but expansive.

During years of facilitating vision and mission statements for clients, at some point during the process I remind the leadership team that the vision is both absolutely necessary and totally insufficient. The vision needs to be lived through the confines of a plan and even—*heaven forbid, no not that, anything but that!*—a budget. Sweeping visions eventually find expression in budgets and the resources connected to them. Most of us have noticed that for visions to happen someone has to order the paper clips and keep toner cartridges in the printer.

Like a company fashioning its mission, individuals responding to their callings express them in the most concrete forms. Such expression is the ultimate human act—to take the limitless and give it limits. In many religions, a core teaching is that God the limitless somehow becomes incarnate, thus saving us from the ignorance, pridefulness, and selfishness that destroy our infinite nature. God saves us from our limits by making our spirits limitless.

The lesson is this:

Spirit needs matter.
High purpose seeks lowly form.
Vision leads to plans.
The unbounded soul wants time and space boundaries.
Answering the call finds expression in the confines of our ordinary lives.

If we don't keep our perspective on this paradoxical union of opposites—the finite and the boundless—then the finite world can destroy the sense of expansiveness that a calling needs. The limits that define our lives—the money we do or don't make, the job titles we live with, the education we do or don't have, the sheer intractability of a problem that won't go away—can shrivel up the sense of having a call, of contributing to something of lasting value.

When soul-shriveling occurs we end up being "realistic," paying attention to the social drummer—"Maybe I should be a food specialist and forget the entrepreneur thing"—losing our capacity to take a path chock-full of soul.

Two famous twentieth-century figures, both with callings, addressed this issue of finding the infinite in the finite. They encouraged our belief in being called by suggesting that humans have the ability to transform the nature of the moment, to break the bounds of space and time and roles, through the attitudes they choose and the beliefs they adopt.

Abraham Maslow, the mid-twentieth-century psychologist of human possibility, saw that the self-actualizing people he studied had turned their careers into vocations (my words, not his), transforming the limits they found in jobs and marriages and life into pools of possibilities.

He even warned against the desire to experience miracles. He saw miracle-seeking as a means to assure the seeker that there is indeed a deeper dimension to life than can be found in the very nonmiraculous ordinary routine in which we spend so much of our time. Looking for miracles in life because you need the excitement and the proof of the extraordinary becomes a dangerous habit. You attribute to an outside source what is possible to find on the inside. His advice, in my paraphrase, is this:

Don't look for miracles. Instead, develop high levels of appreciation and insight because, when viewed with gratitude and freshness, with the eyes of children, everything is miraculous.

Another famous figure who saw the limitless in the limited was Mother Teresa, whose career—when applied to her, doesn't that sound like an abomination—became a world-class vocation. She projected her will on those she served, refusing to see the downtrodden of the earth and instead concentrating on them as children of God. Her calling is a strong reminder of how we transcend the limits of our lives by declaring the limitless possibilities they contain. In a paraphrase of her words:

A calling depends not on how big the actions are that we take; it is about how much love we put into those actions. For God it is all infinite. You do what is small and you do it with love and God will make it infinite.

We will come back to this notion often, and explore more ideas on how to live limitlessly within the everyday limits.

Willing Your Calls into Existence

Mightily believe you have a calling, even as the world is trying to keep you shallow and your circumstances are anything but filled with purpose and significance.

Some people and things in the world will help you find your purpose, but most will not. Ignore, reject, and distance yourself from the parts of society that keep you on the surface of things.

Especially in the flat times, assert your belief in your calling. When there is no evidence of your impact or the significance of what you do, declare your highest intentions.

It is within the confines of the ordinary aspects and roles of your life that your calling is lived. Although you may have a grand set of roles to play in your life, most of us have ordinary roles ready to be injected with meaning and joy if we believe and will our depths into the everyday stuff of life.

In the next chapter, we will examine the negation that comes when you mightily believe in your calling. Believing is the first step; then you will encounter those who don't want you to believe.

Exercise: Heeding Your Inner Voice
and Believing When the Evidence Is Sparse

Here are some questions to help you see if you have listened past the social noise long enough to hear your own callings and to will your way into the deeper aspects of your ordinary roles.

- Have you listened to your inner voice recently?
- Have you . . .
  Gone against a popular opinion?
  Disagreed with your imposing boss? A co-worker?
  Told your parents a truth about yourself?
  Pursued a hobby others thought weird?
  Turned down more money so you could have more meaning?
  Decided not to stay in style?
- Have you looked for the depth dimensions of your ordinary job with its ordinary routines?
- Have you asked, "What does it really mean to be taking the kids to school, to write this report, to analyze this budget, to meet this customer? How can I make this significant?"
- How is your ordinary life laced with meaning, if you allow it to emerge?

Summary

Knowing what a call is, that we have a calling if we rely on our beliefs and not the culture surrounding us, and how to respond to the calls of the lives we find ourselves living, matching them to our penchant for head or heart, or internal or external work—these were the basic lessons of this part of the book.

The called life is not an easier life than other kinds, only a better one. It is better because attempting to do what we are meant for brings the internal joy that can come with commitments that are larger than the confines of our space-bound, time-bound existence. A commitment to a call is not a guarantee of success in the usual way the term is used, as in a career, but it is a guarantee of the success of the self as it decides not to waste life energies on the multiple diversions that we all encounter.

Bob Thompson, a former high-level telecom executive, now off to new things, talks about the hindrances to the call he feels:

> I have a good many hindrances, most of them internal.
>
> I always have a desire for more and better . . . the next best thing is easy to concentrate on, versus the commitment to the real work. We all have this.
>
> Sheer momentum is another one. I had twenty-four years in one industry and had a big job. That can just keep you going.
>
> I was afraid of what others would say when I dropped out and left the successful job.
>
> Just plain fear and doubt. I have kids to send to college. Who knows where this is leading me.

Bob loves music and believes he had a calling. He also is a committed Christian and couldn't stomach the negativity of the music his kids were exposed to daily. So he launched himself into a new orbit to do something positive in music for teens. He didn't know, at the time of our interview, what shape that would take.

But he did know he had a calling

PART II

Breathing Depth
into Common Calls

We are on our way. We have made decisions and have begun or are renewing the responding-to-calls process. The challenges we meet in this phase are different from those in starting up, but no less daunting or rewarding, requiring as much discernment and will.

In this part of the book, we deal with the bad news first. Some people, and even some parts of yourself, will try to divert you from your calls, no matter how hard you have tried to discover and live them. That is the first challenge (chapter 4).

Then we get the good news. You will also find help on the way, as many will nurture your call if you allow it. Your job is to pass the help on, provide support as you can, to those who can use it in their call quest (chapter 5).

Finally, this part of the book deals with the challenge of taking on the bad guys and the conditions they create that make living with purpose harder, sometimes a lot harder, than it needs to be. This is the bad news–good news chapter (chapter 6). In it, we consider the tactics and resolve required to lift spiritual and psychological weights that keep us grounded and spiritually deprived, when we can fly and have call-rich lives if given the chance.

Endure the Saboteurs (4)

THE HINDRANCES [TO ANSWERING MY CALL] EXIST CONTINUOUSLY.
THEY TAKE THE FORM OF PEOPLE, MOSTLY, WHO ARE SO NARROW
IN THEIR EXPERIENCES, CREATIVITY, ENERGIES, AND POSITIVE
THINKING THAT THEY SEE ONLY OBSTACLES IN LIFE.
UNFORTUNATELY, THERE ARE LOTS OF PEOPLE WHO FIT THIS
PROFILE. SUCH PEOPLE CAN DRAIN YOU OF YOUR OWN ENERGIES.

Steve Sheppard
CEO of Foldcraft

IF YOU ARE SERIOUS about answering your call, you will encounter, in the course of your lifetime, people who do not believe in you, who disagree with your purpose, and who resent the part of life that you embody and they do not. The call you spent time and energy discovering and work to answer authentically attracts resistance, encrusted ballast from those who live its opposite.

**Answering a call will bring mentors into your life.
It will also bring tormentors.**

The tormentors are your saboteurs. Although they are to be avoided for as much of your lifetime as possible, they are rarely completely avoidable. For reasons often hard to fathom, in a few key chapters of your life, the saboteurs will play a major role—negating, casting doubt, and destroying your hopes.

If you survive them, you come out tougher and stronger and more attuned to your call than ever. This may be why you attracted them in the first place. If you don't handle their challenge well, the damage can be permanent. And often to your own surprise, the most persistent saboteur in your life can be yourself.

The questions to keep uppermost in mind when dealing with saboteurs are these:

■ How do saboteurs do their work?
■ How can you prepare yourself to see this negation for what it is?
■ What can you learn and how can you benefit from encounters with the forces counter to your calling?
■ What do you do during those times when the worst saboteur you engage is yourself?

HIGH PURPOSE ATTRACTS THE DEMONIC DESTROYERS

If we were sitting around a campfire several centuries ago, we would have heard stories of great knights pursuing noble goals of conquest and protection, and how they would fight to overcome the great and evil intentions of a witch casting a spell or a powerful demon bent on destruction. Or a version of Cinderella might have been told, with the beautiful girl escaping the evil control of her stepmother and cruel sisters.

In contemporary times, the content has changed dramatically but the structure of the stories remains the same. Two generations of children have explored the stories of Luke Skywalker fighting off Darth Vader and discovering his identity. Harry Potter struggles with the evil wizard who took his parents and put the lightning bolt scar on his forehead.

Another such story branded into our memories through a popular book and the myth-making power of Hollywood is *One Flew Over the Cuckoo's Nest*.[1] The reasons for the story's greatness are surely its unlikely, unforgettable hero, McMurphy, and its equally unforgettable villain, Nurse Ratched, whose very name implies her life mission of control, ratcheting whatever she can to the nearest surface so she can keep it from growing into something she can't dominate.

Many of us know the general idea of the Ken Kesey story and some may know the details from many readings of the book or multiple viewings of the movie with a bag of homemade popcorn on a quiet Friday night. But parts of the story bear retelling, especially to illustrate the notion of saboteurs and how they operate to limit people on their way to living out a calling with integrity.

The story is told from the viewpoint of a huge Indian man, the Chief, who pretends throughout to be deaf and dumb. Before McMurphy shows up at the asylum with all those branded psychotic, Nurse Ratched runs her little ward of wounded souls with a perfect mix of medications and group therapy that reminds the patients of how inadequate and ill they are. Her control over them is more important than any healing, and she has long ago decided that her job is to keep them from changing and thus stay in the ward. There, she can see them and they can't cause any trouble.

Into this scene comes a boisterous, partying Irishman, McMurphy, unsocialized to the point of having run-ins with the law fairly commonly and not attached to careers and families like most. Kesey uses the asylum as a microcosm for the world, of course, suggesting that those who are too adjusted to the world have no real life of their own. They are broken in less obvious ways than inmates, surely, but they are still broken. McMurphy may be a meddlesome redheaded Irish rogue, but he would do no one harm. His main goal seems to be to have fun, laugh, and annoy those who can't, which, of course, targets saboteur Ratched from the get-go.

Their battle begins innocently enough. He starts breathing life and spirit into the inmates by laughing and playing and stretching all of the ward's rules. A wild fishing expedition and a ragtag basketball game with his inmate nonathletes are two of the more memorable scenes as McMurphy helps those on the ward enjoy their senses and their bodies again.

Nurse Ratched sees McMurphy for the danger that he is to her system, and so the battle between the saboteur–control freak and the one with the irrepressible human spirit escalates slowly and dramatically to its bitter, triumphant conclusion.

In one scene, McMurphy's will to live and move the immovable is symbolized by his attempt to tear a sink from its stand, literally to rip the plumbing apart with the strength of his muscles multiplied by an indomitable will. After straining with every fiber of his body, the veins nearly bursting through his skin with effort, the sink remains unmoved. But we see, under his party personality, just how fierce the will to live, to go beyond and rip apart everyday constraints, burns at the core of his being.

The battle between McMurphy and Ratched eventually centers around one of the inmates, a stuttering Billie Bibbit, and his struggle to free himself of his sickness and self-doubt. Under McMurphy's influence, the man starts to discover his own mind and questions Nurse Ratched's authority and control. On the fateful night of a big party in the ward, orchestrated by the redhead and attended by some of his party-loving girlfriends, Bibbit rediscovers his manhood. His potency becomes a sign of his return to autonomy and health. His lifelong stammer actually disappears and he can express himself, make up his mind, and have his own opinions as he discovers his own voice.

The morning after the messy party that no one cleaned up, Nurse Ratched comes upon the scene when she enters the ward. This is the last straw—she knows that if her little world is to be maintained she must pull out all the stops. And she is up to the task with a grand moment of sabotage creativity. In her tight-lipped, starchy-nurse-uniform manner, she psychologically castrates the newly potent Bibbit, employing just the right amount of self-disgust-inducing shame—"I'll of course need to tell your mother about this, Billie."

Bibbit is aghast at the thought, and his newly won freedom of mind is too weak to handle this artful attack. He crumbles back into self-doubt and stuttering, and secretly goes to his room where he commits suicide.

When McMurphy absorbs Billie Bibbit's death, he knows the game he is playing with the nurse and her rules is over. He has entered a life-and-death struggle. He attacks Nurse Ratched with his hands on her throat, because her death grip on the inmates has snuffed out a life that mattered to them all. If he had had a few more seconds he might have avenged Bibbit's death, but the guards stop him before he does permanent damage.

He is taken away. The end of the story contains the sad triumph of his will.

McMurphy is seen as dangerous and so, as Nurse Ratched would hope, he is lobotomized; by disconnecting the part of the brain that houses his will, he can no longer cause any trouble. He is now a walking, talking vegetable, with no frontal lobes to make up his own mind about anything.

But the Chief develops a plan. From his pose as mute and deaf, he has silently observed every episode in the grand battle between the human spirit trying to find expression and the saboteur who must squelch everything about the spirit she cannot control. McMurphy's spirit has rekindled his own. The invitation that McMurphy had offered to all the inmates—to throw off the nurse and the medications and the labels and all the institutionalized crud that prevented them from being whole—was initially accepted by Bibbit. Now, when McMurphy is brought back to the ward and put into his bed to sleep, with deep purple scars on his temples, the Chief executes his plan.

He holds a pillow over the Irishman's face to suffocate the body of McMurphy; his soul was already gone. Then he lumbers to the sink that McMurphy had tried to rip apart, leans over it, gets the same grip that McMurphy had a few weeks earlier, and promptly yanks it from its stand. He staggers across the ward supporting its huge mass, and crashes the sink through a screened window. Then he crawls through the window and escapes into the night, never again to let himself be separated from his life force. The spirit that was in McMurphy lives on in the least damaged of the inmates, the Indian who was closest to his roots in nature and whose will has been reactivated.

Saboteur Ratched has done, and will do, more damage, but McMurphy's victory, against huge odds, is for the collective human soul. His resistance to the end was his life force at work, and the Chief's escape is our hope.

LEARNING THE SIGNS AND PATTERNS OF SABOTEURS

The lessons from this classic story about saboteurs and how they operate are important. You may not run into a Nurse Ratched very often in your life. But you may have a coach, a boss, a business partner, a relative—even a spouse—whose main interaction with you squelches your core and muzzles your most vibrant impulses, the ones attached most centrally to your calling.

Businessman Patrick Kelly, CEO of Physician Sales and Service of Jacksonville, Florida, the billion-dollar company that changed the medical supplies delivery business, says that his saboteurs were "bankers and partners. When they didn't see the vision they about killed the company's growth and potential on several occasions."

Philosopher-consultant Peter Koestenbaum relates that his saboteurs were "uncomprehending, disinterested, and invalidating philistine teachers, especially at the university level."

Many of you could name more than one in your life, and all of us have seen saboteurs at work in the lives of others, if not our own.

Knowing when you have a saboteur in your life is the first step in successfully enduring one. Here are the signs of saboteurs at work:

THEY OFTEN LOOK RESPECTABLE AND HAVE AUTHORITY

Nurse Ratched had nursing credentials and years of experience. In some instances saboteurs even are esteemed for their gifts and their contributions.

THEY SPEAK OF POSITIVE MOTIVES TO COUCH THE DAMAGE THEY DO

The best saboteurs are so accomplished at this that they confuse those they are squelching by making it sound as if they are creating and protecting value.

THEY TWIST REALITY

Saboteurs make those who are healthy and life-affirming seem in need of correction and control. They are accomplished at mind games, labeling good things their opposite with such skill and conviction that they go unquestioned.

They Are Masters of Power and Control

By finding the most vulnerable spots in others they know how to employ their tools of shame, anger, or quiet manipulation with measured words. This appeal to weakness becomes the essence of their control over others. The reason why McMurphy was impossible for Nurse Ratched was because he was beyond her control. The power-hold saboteurs gain is the very thing that must be broken for a calling to be lived, just as a wrestler must wriggle his way out of being pinned with both shoulders to the canvas.

They Cause Pain and Enjoy Watching Others Regress

As they busily pursue their own agendas, saboteurs see the pain they inflict on others as a necessary step toward ridding life of unwanted elements.

They Often Do Good in Some Areas of Their Lives

This provides a protective shield for their work of sabotage, confusing even those on the receiving end of the devastation, because the good in other areas is apparent.

The Worst Saboteur in Your Life Is You

Although it is handy to attribute the force of evil to others, the simple truth is that we often do battle with ourselves. We have all been guilty at times not only of squelching the life force that wants to be called in others but even of turning our own worst inclinations against ourselves. We will spend some time on this dark reality later in the chapter, but let's first talk about the need to protect your calling from the saboteur forces embodied in others.

An Early Lesson in Sabotage

I needed to fend off a saboteur in my early career life, and it taught me a valuable lesson.

I have spent most of my working life helping companies and the people in them perform at a higher level, closer to their full potential. In order to become a coach and a consultant, I had to earn my stripes and go through the toils of leading teams and people myself.

In my first-ever supervisory role, my boss's boss had an opening interview with me upon my arrival. I was thirty, energetic, and green, and ready to take on the management role to which I aspired: head of human resources. The forty-something manager had called me into his office, and after I answered a few of his questions, he told me in his deep voice, with a rather toothy smile, that "as I see your background, what you have we don't need, and what we need you don't have."

It wasn't exactly my picture of an encouraging opening meeting with one of my key leaders. I don't know what I said in response, but I got out of the meeting fast and thought about what to do.

I basically did three things. First, when he was around me for the next year, I worked twice as hard to show him why he was wrong. Second, I avoided him whenever I could. Luckily for me, often he was too focused on other issues to bother me. Third, I had an important ally; my immediate boss often ran some effective interference. On occasion, I would ask him to present positions on my behalf and my ideas would go through with much less hassle.

This saboteur's opening comment about what I did and did not have was a shot across the bow that put me on alert. With some judgment and a close ally in my boss, I was able to escape damage to my career and myself. And I was fortunate not to have an advanced saboteur to deal with, only a half-baked one.

A MASTER SABOTEUR

About a decade later a close friend of mine had to endure a saboteur. This one was more serious and focused than the one I had encountered, and I watched my friend—we'll call him Rich—feel some real damage from the experience.

In the course of building his business and offering new services, Rich had come across an especially promising and novel set of empowering management practices that improved business performance while building the talents of the people inside the business. He and his team dedicated themselves to learn, codify, and offer these services to clients everywhere. The services aligned perfectly with the values of Rich and his team, values of empowerment and good business practice. Learning to deliver these services became part of Rich's calling.

To learn and launch this new business Rich created a new ownership team and partnered with a company skilled in the use of the practices and well-known in the marketplace for its accomplishments. The charismatic and powerful leader of this company became Rich's partner, and while things started well enough—as a lot of people with saboteurs for ex-spouses and business partners will tell you—the saboteur colors rose to the surface rather quickly.

First, Rich was warned about how to work with the CEO—we'll call him Blair—by a few of his longtime colleagues. But Rich and his partners didn't listen too well because they were still focusing on the positives. I can remember hearing some of the early glowing reports, and they brushed over Blair's darker side.

Then Rich noticed that Blair had many admirers, but that most of his own people were afraid of him and wouldn't disagree with him. A faint twinge of trepidation could commonly be felt in the room when he questioned others even mildly, and at meetings he would occasionally browbeat others even in front of guests.

During one session, he queried a manager to make a point and left the subordinate manager speechless about his poor judgment. In an audible aside Blair said, "Can you picture how that guy taught us to filet those fish we catch, how to debone them with just a few strokes of the knife?" He let the question hang over the room as the metaphor for what he had just done to the manager, letting it soak into everyone's imagination. Blair was the master of the filet, cutting his own managers if he decided they needed it.

After a company manager who reported to Blair had to endure a public questioning some months later, the next manager to have to report was physically ill at ease and rushed back to her seat, clearly hoping that by sitting down and disappearing she would avoid a public question. It was both somehow humorous—a few people laughed— and sad to see a competent, grown woman reduced to a childlike state, scurrying from potential punishment.

Blair ran his kingdom well, sometimes very unobtrusively—like Nurse Ratched—because the rules had been put into place and his minions enforced them. He could often be funny and joyful and insightful. And he often performed kind acts, genuinely helping many with his educating style. But he made sure his inner circle knew how much he sacrificed and how and when he had been heroic.

The technique he used most often on Rich and his partners, and especially on Rich as the chief liaison in the partnership, was what they called "letting him go until he self-destructs." In this saboteur game, only the most formal contact was maintained while someone was given a job to do. Then, all feedback, support, and substantive contact would be withdrawn until the person was filled with self-doubt and couldn't perform.

Rich saw Blair do the self-destruct dance with others before him and did not understand it fully at first. After about ten months into the deal, Blair cut Rich and his colleagues off from any serious contact. Blair's team needed no coaching on how to proceed, being practiced in it, and they stepped in line to move from partnering to a kind of friendly shunning. In the meantime, Blair and his team made it known that they wanted other partners "to fill out their service options." This in effect negated Rich's partnership. But Blair had covered himself in the best saboteur style—he could simply say the partnership hadn't worked because Rich and his colleagues self-destructed.

There are more Blair stories, of course: how he used anger, how he'd absorb others' contacts and make them his own, how he couldn't accept feedback. When Rich gave him feedback on a few occasions, he would argue back, and instead of trying to learn from the feedback would try to fix things with some manipulation of the work process. He would usually delegate "the problem," as he saw it, to someone else so he would not have to bother changing anything about himself. In his mind, he was a small part of the problem at most, and others had to get it together.

Rich saw Blair repeat the pattern with others who followed, beautiful variations on the same saboteur pattern as he'd find a flaw and play on it until the relationship ended.

Much of Rich's insight into Blair came after some time had passed. During the interactions it was an often-confusing mix of polite and minimal interaction, and because of the self-destruct policy, lack of meaningful contact. The lack of feedback is very disconcerting, of course, because in a start-up with little positive market feedback to count on initially, the interaction with a partner is crucial. The shunning was crazy-making in the extreme, a great saboteur method for creating self-doubt.

THE DAMAGE SABOTEURS INFLICT

Blair's full impact on Rich, as an early forty-something with a good string of successes, was broad and long-lived. Because of intense persistence on Rich's part, the partnership went on for three years. Blair's minions actually began to admire Rich because no one had lasted even half the time. He felt so committed to the value his team could provide clients that he endured financial difficulties and Blair's abuses in order to continue to learn the skills and bring value to the marketplace. This work had truly become part of his calling.

But by his account, here is the damage the relationship with Blair caused him:

- *Raging self-doubt and negation.* For months and parts of years the success and good work he had done were pushed far into the background. He wondered if he had really acquired skills and added value.
- *Persistent overworking to prove a point.* He took his tendency to overcommit to an extreme. He overinvested time and energy and money at the expense of life balance on many occasions.
- *Questioning of values.* He would wonder if the values he held were of any real substance in the world, or if he was just wasting his time.
- *Occasional use of some of Blair's tactics.* He got so good at seeing what Blair was doing to others that on a few occasions he forgot himself and retaliated with some of the same hurtful tactics, once with Blair himself and once with one of his reports.
- *Obsessive clinging to a few straws.* The lack of feedback clouded his judgment, and instead of seeing things for what they were he desperately clung to a few shreds of positive feedback, far outweighing their true value.

The wounds healed with some visible scars left. But years after the damage began, if I get him to tell me the stories, Rich can still bring back certain memories that generate anger and pain. The breadth of the damage is matched by its enduring nature.

**Use the saboteur to grow more deeply committed to your calling.
Extract value from your saboteur encounters.**

LESSONS TO LEARN

In a review of what he learned as a whole from this encounter with the saboteur, Rich drew several lessons, the universal kind that anyone facing a saboteur can relate to. In fact, if you can extract learning from enduring them, saboteurs serve many useful purposes.

One of the key things saboteurs teach is exactly how you don't want to be. After a serious encounter with one, most of us take a vow, a solemn vow: "If I ever get to a position like that, I will never, e-v-e-r, do to somebody else what he did to me!!"

Remembering your saboteur, keep in mind the lessons listed here that most apply to you.

TOUGHEN UP

The pain and stress of enduring a saboteur becomes easier if you use the experience to reaffirm your values and the calling you are attempting to give expression to. It is easy to have a calling when all goes well; it is far harder and of longer-term value to commit to it while you are being negated.

Getting thicker-skinned at some earlier stage will help you endure the other debunkers and negaters who are sure to come later.

WEAKEN YOUR WEAKNESS

The saboteur is effective in part because he can exploit a weakness. When you see, for example, that your tendency to let others' opinions matter too much or to take everything a person says at face value are weaknesses that will continue to limit you, you owe it to your calling, if not to yourself, to lessen that tendency's hold on you. You will have no better motivation than after the souring and lingering encounters with a saboteur to do something about yourself.

ALWAYS REMEMBER THE SABOTEUR'S NEGATIVE IMPACT ON YOU

Never forget the self-doubt and negation, so that you never let yourself feel or think that again. One lesson from an encounter with a saboteur is the realization that you cooperated with the control he or she had over you. By remembering that lesson, you never let it happen again.

WHEN YOU BREAK OUT OF THE SABOTEUR'S GRIP, GIVE YOURSELF SOME HEALING TIME

The damage done by a saboteur will take some time to repair. Don't put yourself on too fast a track to get back to the healthier you. And don't be surprised if you never totally get over it. The memory of the pain may always be there, under the surface.

FORGIVE

One of the more damaging long-term impacts of an encounter with a saboteur can be to leave you cynical, doubting others' motives, and too ready to see the minor sabotaging flaws that reside in all of us. Muster up the intellectual judgment to forgive the saboteur, and with the gift of time and some regular doses of prayer, most likely your emotional forgiveness will follow. Forgiveness washes away the bitterness, leaves you free to move ahead with your calling, and keeps you just as vigilant against saboteurs of any stripe in your future.

GIVE OTHERS THE BENEFIT OF YOUR INSIGHT

Help others in the grip of a saboteur to see what they are letting themselves go through. A person who has endured a saboteur can teach others who can't see them for what they are. Be an anchor for those who are stuck, inform them of the reality of a partner like Blair or a Nurse Ratched in their lives.

FIGHTING YOUR SABOTEUR SELF: THE ULTIMATE BATTLE

As grand as the stories of pitched battles between strong evils and courageous goods are, the grandest stories of all are of people conquering their own internal saboteur, the one that limits both others and themselves.

It would be simpler if life were so clear and bounded that we could ascribe all evil to others and view our own intentions and actions as always noble, always fair. But with maturity we learn that when things go bad we often had a part to play in the mess. A divorce is not the fault of one, but of two. A dashed business partnership ending in legal haggling also involves two parties, not one.

Just as often, when you start the good fight against the saboteur who is limiting your life, you discover that the real enemy is you. The only reason the saboteur coach or boss or teacher is able to dampen your spirit is because you are dampening it yourself with your own belief system and mental patterns.

One of the saboteur's skills, you'll remember, is finding and exploiting a weakness. We have such weaknesses because we haven't taken care of that part of ourselves yet. A feature of our mental or emotional model of the world and our place in it isn't complete and whole.

Bob Thompson, the telephone company executive we met earlier, had big doubts about his decision to become an entrepreneur in the music business and give kids better musical choices, something he felt called to do. "I worried about what others would think, and I had really only known business success, so I had this tremendous momentum going. Most of all, my pessimism in moving ahead to new work showed up as realism. . . . That was my biggest challenge, knowing that the realistic side of me always served me well, but my pessimism disguised itself as realism in this instance."

One of the tricks is to remember that your weaknesses are tied to your strengths:

- You are a natural helper, but you give of yourself too much.
- You are a fine achiever, but you can't stand to lose.
- You take charge as a matter of course, but you limit others by having to keep control.

This juxtaposition of strength and weakness is the reason we avoid working on ourselves. We focus on the good part, "I am so caring" (taking the first of the three preceding examples) and find it handy to push into denial the flip side of this feature, "I overnurture others and get taken advantage of."

As long as we stay in denial and refuse to work on ourselves, we attract people into our lives to exploit this weakness. The saboteur in us colludes with the external saboteur in our lives and together they deliver oodles of pain to the psyche: "Oh, I loved so much. I even showed my love by giving her all my money and extra time." And when she leaves, without appreciation for our overgiving, we hurt intensely, smashed by the experience. The smashing and the pain can make us cynical and protective, negating the part of us that responds to a call of human connection and caring.

This is how self-sabotage occurs. The essential you is working hard to express your real values and purpose, and the saboteur in you finds ways to create the illusion that caring can't work.

Sabotaging Yourself on the Team

I have seen an ugly dynamic often develop on management teams with this shadow-collusion as its base. An overly verbal peer on the team, commonly with a slightly too-high opinion of herself, faces a huge amount of work with her team, made up primarily of less verbal, reserved personalities. As the tension of the work builds, she gets louder, makes more decisions, takes up most of the airtime at meetings, and her teammates get more frustrated, shut down, say less, and contribute little to what becomes "her show." The cycle of poor dynamics gets reinforced by everyone not willing to work on their undeveloped part. She needs to learn some humility and listening skills, and the others need to speak up and not be afraid of conflict.

Instead, they focus on what is outside of them, the lousy team or the loudmouthed peer, because it is easier to do that than to confront their own inner saboteurs with whom they have comfortably lived for as long as they can remember.

This is a two-way, self-sabotaging street that makes it look like an outer saboteur is at work but is about inner saboteurs in equal measure.

We unconsciously recruit many of our saboteurs.

Because we can't do the necessary learning ourselves, we actively go out and find the saboteurs, without being aware of it. We can't see our weakness or flaw for what it is and we are too afraid to admit it and name it for what it is. So, to move us off our lack of insight, we need more pain and frustration as a motivation. We look hard for the right saboteurs, custom fit to have all the right-wrong qualities and drive us berserk. Then, and often only then, when we are in enough pain to do something about it, do we muster up the will to move on and grow.

We need a foil, an enemy, an external embodiment of the part of us that is limiting our growth on the path. With a raging saboteur in our lives, tromping all over our neediest, limiting parts, we can no longer deny our self-limiting tendencies. With an external force causing the pain, we eventually recognize the work we have to do, the work we have been avoiding. The work and effort and will to fend off the saboteur creates the inner resolve and capability needed to pursue our calling.

We will spend more time on fighting the ego, one of whose gambits is to be an inner saboteur, in chapter 7. For now it is only important to recognize that the battle against an external enemy is a battle to claim a part of yourself.

In the end, the way you deal with saboteurs, either inner or outer, is to outlast them. Endure them. Persist and wear them out. Then assess the damage, heal yourself as best you can, and minimize the bitterness, a quality that can taint your response to your calling.

And do the best thing. Take the lessons you have learned and move on.

After an encounter with a saboteur you will see many more possibilities to live your calling. You'll be wiser, and most probably, a lot tougher.

Overcoming the Inevitable Negation of Your Call

Endure the saboteurs, because you will be tested and negated by those who don't want you to live with a purpose and act on your particular calling.

Learn the methods that saboteurs use in their quest for control. Pay special attention to the weakness in your mental or emotional makeup that they play on so you can see how the principles they espouse—innocent and even noble-sounding for the most part, ones you can agree with—disguise the destructive nature of their work.

Extract value from your encounters with saboteurs. Move on with a greater-than-ever sense of purpose, with a capability to sniff out saboteurs in the early stages.

Forgive and move on the wiser for your encounter. Help others endure their saboteur episodes with the knowledge you've gained and the patterns you can predict.

Take a good long look at how you have been your own worst saboteur by denying there are parts of you that need strengthening. The saboteurs who make your life so difficult, unwittingly invited there by you, teach you what you need to work on.

EXERCISE: REFLECTING ON SABOTEURS AND THEIR IMPACT

- How many saboteurs have you fought off in the past or are in the process of currently outlasting?
- What long-term damage have you suffered in the process?
  Ongoing bitterness?
  Damage to your confidence and self-esteem?
  Doubts about your worth and purpose and direction?
  Loss of ability to take risks?
  Cynicism about the human condition?
  Abandonment of something you love?
- What can you do to control the damage and move on? See a therapist? Have some conversations with friends? Do some journaling? Hire a coach?
- What long-term gains and lessons have you learned that you are passing on to others?
- How do you sabotage yourself?
- What saboteurs did you attract into your life so you could heighten the pain level and start working on the undeveloped parts of yourself?

Pass On the Evocateur's Gift ⑤

TO LIVE CONTENT WITH SMALL MEANS
TO SEEK ELEGANCE RATHER THAN LUXURY, AND REFINEMENT RATHER THAN FASHION
TO BE WORTHY, NOT RESPECTABLE, AND WEALTHY, NOT RICH
TO STUDY HARD, THINK QUIETLY, TALK GENTLY, ACT FRANKLY
TO LISTEN TO THE STARS AND BIRDS, TO BABES AND SAGES WITH OPEN HEART
TO BEAR ALL CHEERFULLY, DO ALL BRAVELY, AWAIT OCCASIONS, HURRY NEVER
IN A WORD,
TO LET THE SPIRITUAL UNCONSCIOUS AND UNBIDDEN GROW UP
THROUGH THE COMMON.

William Henry Channing

YOU HAVE COME some distance in answering your call. You believe intensely that you have a calling, and you have escaped the clutches of a saboteur or two. The good news is that people who have identified their calls don't just attract saboteurs, they also attract supporters.

CALLING FORTH POTENTIAL

When you find support for your call in the form of people who take the time to assist your development, you begin the work of adding value to the world by becoming more of who you are. In this chapter we explore how assistance often comes in the form of dedicated others. Providing this assistance in and of itself is a type of calling.

People who provide assistance have a common characteristic: they see past the routine flow of events and people and sense the deeper issues at work. They see "the spiritual unconscious and unbidden," as the epigraph to this chapter by Channing puts it. They then take it upon themselves to help those around them to see these essential possibilities, both the ones just beneath the surface and those more deeply buried.

A person who expresses this talent we will call an *evocateur*—one who evokes out of people and their circumstances the skills, gifts, and potential they did not know they had. The word evocateur comes from the Latin *ex*, which means outside of, and *vocis*, to call. An *e*(x)-*vocateur* is someone, then, who calls to the outside, who calls forth that which was within.

The etymological root of evocateur is the same as vocation, which we described earlier. People with a calling have gone beyond their careers, beyond the roles that society provides them, beyond the social noise that demands they fit in and consume. By evoking that which lurks under the surface, by calling forth that which is embedded in the everyday, an evocateur shows others how the journey to their destiny is possible. How this calling forth of hidden potential comes about is worth investigation.

More questions for answering your call arise as we think about the types of support we have received:

- What can you learn from those who have permanently touched your life with their support? How did they help you grow?
- What is it that you can tap in yourself and others that helps you and them become more than they currently are?
- How can you pass on the gift, the one that you were given, of soul activation and becoming prepared for your callings?

THE COACH AND THE NO-DRIBBLE, NO-SHOOT POINT GUARD

I have encountered many evocateurs in my life, some great and some small—people who invited me to take the next step, large or not, in realizing and living my potential. Anyone who has ever had a mentor knows what it's like to experience an evocateur.

I choose to tell the story of an evocateur I encountered in my early teens because it includes so many of the essential elements of how evocateurs work. And I tell it because as I see mommies and daddies across the land taking their kids to soccer and basketball practice, I know that a lot of evoking is going on. During an ordinary Saturday morning game or match, some essential dimensions of being human are being called forth.

When I was fourteen I had mixed self-confidence. I got good grades in all my academic subjects, but then there were sports. Basketball was becoming my favorite sport—and I played them all, thanks to a father who loved sports—but I had developed a raging case of performance anxiety. Some kids get uptight when tested academically. I got uptight in games and important practice situations. The evidence: although I was as good as the rest of the kids on the playground, I scored a total of two points in two years of playing on the seventh- and eighth-grade teams at Holy Cross School on the near south side of Omaha, Nebraska. My love of basketball and lots of playing didn't produce much.

My father got transferred to Cheyenne, Wyoming, to continue his training as a federal executive in the summer after eighth grade. So when I tried out for the freshman basketball team at my new high school, I wasn't exuberant about my chances to do much on the team.

The good news was that at St. Mary's High School, the only Catholic high school in the state not tied to an Indian reservation (it has since closed), there weren't very many kids. So any warm, breathing body could make the team. I don't remember anyone being cut.

We had a memorable coach that year—a six-foot four-inch, slender, early-thirty-something salesman by trade by the name of Jim Robey. Coach Robey, as we called him, had played some pretty good basketball in his day at Oklahoma City University, which had made a name for itself in the 1950s with its program. What made him memorable for my teammates and me was that he was a skilled evocateur.

Coach Robey often was unshaven—we noticed his stubble on his thin face, very unlike our clean-shaven dads. His eyes sparkled a lot, and he liked to laugh. He did the usual amount of yelling and cajoling that coaches do. What made the yelling tolerable was that he kidded us a lot and had fun—we knew his yelling was more about intensity than anything. He liked to run a lot of drills before we scrimmaged. He had no doubt noticed that we needed a lot of work on the fundamentals.

Coach Robey was realistic in his assessment of the talent, and in many cases the lack thereof, that he had inherited. Before games when he knew we were facing far superior talent, our goal was not to win but to improve some aspect of our offense or defense. Through his realism we could walk away from defeats with some learning and some pride in our improvement.

As the weeks went by, Coach Robey noticed something that was more than a little detrimental to my play. Since I was only five-foot-three, he had made me a point guard, third-string point guard. But I had a little problem: I was nervous with the ball in my hands and I'd get rid of it as soon as possible on all occasions. A point guard without the ball is a problem. Since handling the ball is a central skill for this position, Robey pulled me to the side more than once, which wasn't that easy because our gym was so small—one of the backboards was actually attached to a wall—and assured me I could dribble just fine and that I should not be so eager to pass.

I took his words to heart; I was a coachable kid.

As our season wore on with a bit more than 50 percent wins, more than our talent alone could account for, it was clear that we were better coached and drilled than most of our opponents, and we had a system with real options for both defense and offense. Our little team, the St. Mary's Gaels, would wheel across half of Wyoming for a game or two—a state with only half a million people spread all over mountains and high prairie demanded long trips. Which, when you are fourteen, is part of the fun.

I didn't play much in the games but that did not stop Robey from giving me and the other non-first-stringers some individual attention. He noticed another thing about my game that was hurting my performance. I had very little confidence shooting. I'd pass up all but the most open shots, even short ones, passing to someone I was sure would score more effectively than I could. So we had another little talk on the side of the court one day.

"You've got to put the ball in the hole," Robey insisted. (That was the equivalent of "shoot the rock" in today's terminology.) "The offense needs you to score and to shoot on some of those plays. You can distribute the ball and shoot too."

I was a coachable kid, so in the scrimmages I started taking some more shots.

Then I had a practice on a night toward the end of the season that has gone down in my memory. I couldn't miss. Everything I put up went in, and I put up a lot of shots for a change. At one point I took what today would be the equivalent of a long three-pointer; I winced a little at my recklessness—how could I take such a long shot? The ball hit nothing but net. I was hot.

After I made the long shot, as I ran down the court to play defense, Robey saw I was all aglow and obviously still relishing the shot. Robey seized the moment. Like all good evocateurs, he could see that the student was ready for a message. He knew that the potential he had been coaxing out of me a little at a time could now make a big leap. In my agitated state, he could implant a new message. The moment presented him with the opportunity that evocateurs live for.

Robey cupped his hands over his mouth and yelled across the gym at me: "Schuster, what'd I tell you—*you're a shooter!*"

It was as if my back had a steel band that went up and down just inside the skin, and Robey's proclamation reverberated the length of my spine like a jolt of jagged lightning. Waahh . . . waahh . . . waahh went the jolt. I can still feel it almost four decades later.

At that moment, in the little gym at St. Mary's, a shooter was born.

It happened by decree, apparently, as Coach Robey assumed some magical power to declare my identity. In the remaining weeks of the season, with my newfound confidence, I actually scored some points in every game we played. As adolescent hormones rush and churn, I grew seven inches the next year. I was the leading scorer on the junior varsity the next year and started on the varsity the one after that.

LASTING MEMORIES, LASTING LESSONS

Fast-forward four decades. To this day, as I live and breathe in the second half of my life here in the twenty-first century, on most Sunday nights, with my buddies and some of our twenty-something kids and nephews, I still play ball. It isn't like the ball we used to play. It's not very pretty, this older, white-man type of basketball, with very few offensive moves. Rebounding and shooting are about all that is left. But many years after the practice in which I couldn't miss, I still shoot with confidence. When I have a bad night, I know I'll come back the next time.

The work of evocateurs usually lasts a while.

At our end of the season party back in 1963, Coach Robey arranged for a little celebration of his own design. The school couldn't afford trophies and he maybe earned $200 for his entire season's pay, but out of his own pocket he got each kid on the team a little trophy, the three-inch-high variety with a plastic basketball figure on top of a wood base. The plastic was painted gold, which started to chip on the way home from the party and was half gone by the time I lost it during one of my many moves ten or twenty years later.

Each trophy had a few words composed by Coach Robey taped on the base—engraving was out of the question. The first strings got what they deserved: Ace Evans, the highest scorer, Mike McDill the most rebounds and the beginning of a basketball career that would take him to the Air Force Academy on scholarship, Gerry Tomlin, the most assists, and so on. When he got to the lesser players, Robey kept going with his acknowledgments of our unique, if not so noteworthy, contributions.

I still remember mine. Affixed to my trophy were these words—

Best Question Asker

Now that's reaching a bit.

But sure enough, it was true. During the practices, as we were working our systems and getting shots for this guy rolling off of that pick or passing to the second player through, I'd raise my hand and ask why this and why that. Coach Robey noticed, and he liked the fact that my head was in the game.

I've had other mentors and evocateurs in my life. As I went on to teach high school, create a consulting business, and coach executives, I remember as much as any the call that touched me as a high school kid. Coach Robey had probably never attended a seminar on how to get people to do their best. Who knows how much he thought about having a calling, and surely he never thought about being an evocateur.

What Robey loved was basketball and kids, and the rest came to him naturally. He did what he did for a reason—to make a contribution in some way. He answered his call to coach. *"You're a shooter!"* That moment was identity-forming. It showed me as clearly as all the events of the first third of my life how people can evoke the skill and potential of other people that lie dormant, waiting to be released.

TAPPING THAT WHICH LIES DORMANT

How did Robey, a coach I had for five months as an early adolescent, make such an impact? How do evocateurs like him operate? What do they think, and what do they do to call forth all that latent energy and capacity?

They do several things.

EVOCATEURS SOAK UP REALITY AND TELL THE TRUTH

Although evocateurs work at bringing to the surface what has not yet arrived there, they don't make the debilitating mistake of dreaming that reality is something other than what it is. They work from the hard facts and accept them as the facts, not something to wish away. Robey, like other coach evocateurs, had success because he worked with what he had and set realistic goals—like to improve rather than to win against the obviously more gifted.

EVOCATEURS SEE WHAT OTHERS SEE, BUT THEY THINK SOMETHING DIFFERENT

If evocateurs see reality, they concentrate on potential. They are gifted in understanding people, hearing what people say and then listening to what was meant. They hear the subscript of deeper meaning behind the words and actions. Evocateurs live in the subscript, in the deeper computer language behind the software. In this way, they may observe what others do but they think under the surface, at the core, the essence, the seed level.

EVOCATEURS APPEAL TO THE INNATE HUMAN LONGING TO BE MORE THAN WE ARE

My former partner, Tom Stevenin, often used to close his speeches with one of his favorite old poems:

> Three women walked down the road, did she
> The one she was
> The one they saw
> And the one that she wanted to be

As the old poem indicates (and if anyone knows the source, please let me know—I lost it some years ago) the reality of who the woman is differs from what others think she is. And both of those differ from who she hopes to become. Evocateurs live in the realm of what we hope to become.

EVOCATEURS BOTH FIND AND CREATE TEACHABLE MOMENTS

Steve Sheppard writes about his evocateur:

I began to recognize other possibilities in the workplace: I experienced how a more ethical and caring approach to running a business could create success. . . .

I give credit for this awakening to Foldcraft founder Harold Nielsen, who was and is still the most out-of-the-box thinker I have ever known. Harold allowed me to be myself and to leverage whatever strengths I might have had to my advantage as well as the company's advantage. He pushed me in some directions I would never have followed on my own. He gave me great confidence. I think I had to be willing to take some personal risks along the way, but Harold was the one providing the opportunities.

Harold's pushing and providing teachable moments were the essence of the growth process that Steve lived as he led the exciting social experiment of Foldcraft from his CEO position.

EVOCATEURS ADAPT THEIR METHOD

Dorothy Delay, the great Julliard School violin teacher during the last half of the twentieth century, had one of her students say this about her: "She can look at a student and figure out in a very short period of time how to get into here [pointing at her head]. She figures out how *they* think. And that is her method—that she has no method."

Coach Robey worked with my performance anxiety in a much different way than he worked with my teammate, Ace Evans, who had an overconfidence challenge, or Mike McDill, who was working on coordination. Evocateurs know when to push and prod, when to celebrate, when to answer a student's question with a question, and when to give a directive.

EVOCATEURS WORK AT THE LEVEL OF IDENTITY

Evocateurs use many methods, but all are aimed at transforming their student's understanding of what it means to be a person. Their work advances skill and shapes capability, but their fundamental lessons are about who a person is, what his mission is, what purpose he wants to serve.

I became a shooter under Robey, but the experience affected my self-confidence and my learning about how I wanted to help people grow into their gifts. Steve Sheppard became a businessman, and with his mentor's guidance, the CEO of a company. But mostly, he became more of a person.

EVOCATEURS ACKNOWLEDGE

Evocateurs call forth by naming, affirming, acknowledging what a person is or has or will be.

The behavioral psychologists call positive consequences for behavior *reinforcement*. Reinforcement is powerful and is connected to evoking, but doesn't go deep enough. Evoking is to name the essence of what is, before it is fully realized, so the person can grow into that identity.

"You are a shooter!"
"You are a compassionate and highly competent CEO!"
"You are a violin soloist!"
"You are a _____!" (Just fill in the blank.)

These declarations by the evocateur awaken the will of the student or colleague.

The will of those being evoked, the identity that is coming into being, aligns with the will of the evocateur through the act of acknowledgment, receiving an adrenaline boost of human intentionality.

Acknowledging is the essence of the evocateur's creative alignment with the calling of another. Acknowledging the deepest longing of another to grow is the essence of the evocateur's call.

A WRITER'S EVOCATEUR

I want to continue with my high school period for one more example, but I shift to a new chapter and a friend in a new city.

Toward the end of my junior year at St. Mary's, my father got a promotion and the family moved east to Cincinnati. I had a rough transition, the only one in all the moves we had made, and it had to do with being sixteen rather than younger.

But by fall of my senior year, some six months after the move, I was making new friends. One of the more important ones was a kid like none other by the name of Dave Quammen, the one I quoted at the end of the first chapter as the writer answering his call: "I sit down at the computer with a cup of coffee at 8 A.M., blink once, become mesmerized, blink again, and it's 6 P.M., the coffee is half-drunk, my shirt is drenched with sweat, and maybe, maybe, I have three pages of workable, fixable first draft. This is ecstasy. This is life."

That one, if you remember.

Dave taught me mah-jongg and tennis, liked different music, always had his head in a book, and usually said things in ways no one else would say or think them.

But before "Q," as we called and still call him, became a writer's writer, before he won awards or became a Rhodes scholar or spent fifteen years writing the "Natural Acts" column for *Outside Magazine,* or went on tour lecturing about losing species across the globe, before he traveled to the Amazon or retraced the steps of nineteenth-century naturalists into the South Seas, before he had figured out how to yoke his love of science and nature to his gifts and passion for writing, before any of that took place, he had to encounter an evocateur to acknowledge and call forth his gifts.

We had an English teacher in our senior year at all-boys St. Xavier High School. This man had gone to Oxford, wore a beret, and excelled at being a crusty forty-something with a passion for literature, nasty cigars, and sherry. He was the best and most demanding teacher any of us had ever had. He taught us new ways to think and he insisted that we write lots of essays in class. He opened up the worlds of literature and art and metaphor. For those of you into pop culture, if you saw Robin Williams in *Dead Poets Society,* this teacher, Fr. Thomas Savage, Jesuit, was our Robin Williams. He turned us on to our own minds and the gifts of literature and read the *carpe diem* poem, if you remember the intense scene from the movie.

It was the late sixties and Vietnam and racism and civil rights were exploding into our living rooms and "Sav," as he became known, was one of our intellectual anchors, one of our headlights for finding our way in the darkness of a world that didn't inspire much confidence but did generate healthy doses of cynicism.

For Q, Sav was the first and deepest and most lasting of the evocateurs to affirm his talent and give it shape.

Here is Q talking about Sav.

If I had a role model at age seventeen, I suppose it was Tommy Smothers or Randy Sparks [the latter, producer-leader of the New Christie Minstrels]. Ugh. Thank God for Thomas G. Savage. If I had a biology teacher as inspiring as him, I'd probably be a tropical ecologist right now with a research site in the Ecuadorean Amazon and a pile of unpublished popular essays (or maybe a novel, God forbid) in my desk drawer.

Sav was the one who said in 1966, "Why don't you think about Yale, not just Boston College and Holy Cross?"

"Why Yale?" I asked.

"Because it's got the best English department in the country," said Savage.

"What's so great about its English department?" said I.

"Well, they've got Penn Warren, for starters," said Sav. [For those of you who don't read literature, Warren was a man of letters who won the Pulitzer Prize for All the King's Men, *the classic novel based on Huey Long that was made into a mediocre Hollywood movie with Broderick Crawford, among other accomplishments.]*

So it was Sav first, who encouraged me to aspire beyond the pious conventional boundaries.

I asked Q, after he gave several more responses, if he had any other thoughts. He added this: "Have I mentioned that Thomas G. Savage was the greatest teacher and sweetest man who ever lived? If I ever shot a movie about fate and muse, the guardian angel would wear a black beret, a Roman collar, and smoke cigars like old tarred rope."

That would be Q's tribute to his main evocateur, and hundreds of other Xavier students' main one as well.

GIFTS SURFACED: PASSING IT ON

The best part of Coach Robey and my love for basketball is not what it has done for my health or my high school glory years. It's what is still going on now.

I became a father in my midtwenties and I passed my love of the game on to my two sons, who still let me play with them on occasion. The older son has coached a seventh-grade team in Ohio and poured his energy and personality into it. The younger son played on a team that was state-ranked and turned out college players. (My grandson, Micah, sent me a picture of him—all four feet of him—in a uniform holding a "bakaball." He shoots regularly on his seven-foot basket and watches NBA tapes of master slam dunks with his parents.) My sons have healthy confidence derived from many aspects of their lives, but which was helped by mastering aspects of a game. They enjoy physical activity and have a love of healthy competition.

These boys, at best, however, have only a distant awareness of a coach who gave extra time and attention, forty years ago and thirteen hundred miles away, to the younger, nervous version of their dad.

That happens with time and generations.

But that's OK. That is how calls make their impact.

The work of evocateurs lasts a long time, longer than the memories of the people they affect or the generations following.

The invitations for developing beyond our current limitations pop up unexpectedly, happen, and then disappear. The spurts of growth and deep identity-building that come from evocateur co-workers, teachers, coaches, parents, friends, aunts, uncles, and bosses are often lost by those who do the growing, let alone their kids. Life enfolds in its past a blur of memory fragments and misty knowings, and we realize that we didn't become who we are by accident. We are able to attribute some specific talent and qualities to certain evocateurs, events, and influences. But we don't hold onto them all.

For every Coach Robey I remember, for every Thomas G. Savage, whose callings had such an impact, I'm sure there are others I don't remember.

It's the memories we do have that matter, and the attitude that we assume for those we have forgotten. The attitude that seems most useful is one of gratitude for all the formative moments, for all the *"You're a shooter!"* happenings that make up our life. Those who activated something of lasting value in us may not all be remembered, but they must be honored.

We are all self-made, but not without a thousand life-altering impacts we absorb along the way. Honoring those whose lessons have helped shape our identities increases the chances that we will pass on the invitation to grow to others.

The requirement to pass on the invitation is obvious. Once you reflect on how you were on the receiving end of evocateurs' invitations and activations, you are capable of passing on the same gift. By remembering what they provided, and how, you see the opportunities to do the same for those in need of the activations you can provide.

Increasing the total number of invitations and activations is the task before us all. It is our collective calling.

In the final chapter of the book we will delve more into the practices of evocateurs. In the next chapter we discuss the unique call that creates the conditions that allow evocateurs to do their work.

Potential Everywhere

Learn how others *evoke the possibilities* that they see. The world needs realism as its foundation, and it needs the calling forth of potential as its hope for the future.

The practices of the evocateur are fundamental to finding and providing the needed support for answering a call to meaning and purpose. Calling forth potential through declaration and affirmation is an act of human will that can happen even in the routine aspects of life.

Practice seeing the potential beneath the surface. The universal yearning to become is the force that evocateurs tap. By cooperating with this yearning they coax potential into reality. Extending this invitation to grow as often as possible ensures that more of us can access our inner authority and live our possibilities.

Pass on the invitation, spread the gift.

EXERCISE: DEEPENING YOUR APPRECIATION OF EVOCATEURS' IMPACT ON YOUR LIFE

- Who has been an evocateur in your life?
- What dimension or dimensions of you did they call forth?
- How did they do it? What methods did they use and what teachable moments did they create or seize?
- How are you being asked to be an evocateur in your life now?
- How have you been one in the past, and what are you hopes for your future of calling forth potential?

Provoke the Stifling 6

AT TIMES, people face circumstances they feel compelled to challenge. They direct themselves to attack intensely the way things are because the sum of those things, or one aspect they find particularly appalling, is destroying human possibilities.

This work constitutes a special kind of calling, one that takes courage in the face of organized adversity. If *evocateurs* evoke potential and capability, then those who challenge the injustice of a system, provoking its members to abandon the current design, must be named provocateurs. While many people bravely endure and personally triumph over injustice, fewer devote themselves to eliminating the injustice for themselves, for others, and for future generations. This is the calling of the provocateur.

Most of us have the need and the opportunity to be a provocateur at some stage or time in our lives. We know that something isn't right and needs to be addressed. In business settings, the stifling of the human spirit continues even though we have sponsored three decades of new business practices in participation and teaming that were aimed at enlivening the spirit. This kind of nonprogress leads strategy guru Gary Hamel to write:

> We were promised relief from tedium; we got the white-collar factory. We were promised a degree of autonomy; we got binders full of corporate policies. We were promised a sense of true purpose; we got the tyranny of quarterly returns. We were promised the chance to contribute; we got endless meetings where form regularly beat substance to a pulp. . . . We were often called "associates" but were as expendable as worn-out machines.[1]

Good provoking of the corporate status quo, wouldn't you say? Hamel captures our disgust at the shallowness of our change efforts.

(Hamel's earlier work on strategy concentrated on the systems that sustain innovation, but as he looked at business innovation more carefully it appears he shifted to the realization that individuals answering their call to buck complacency, provocateurs all, were more important than any system a business can put in place to ensure innovation.)

This unique kind of call, an inbred antagonism for the status quo, raises important questions:

- How do provocateurs effectively carry out their role?
- What pitfalls do provocateurs need to avoid in living out this difficult calling?
- How can you sponsor other provocateurs when you know your time for this type of call is past?

BATTLES FOUGHT

The stifling practices provocateurs battle happen everywhere, throughout all human history, and in every human endeavor, a few of which I list in the following paragraphs. What they have in common is that the stifling constitutes a moral if not legal injustice that blocks human potential and freedom.

A brief description of several provocateurs will remind us of how important this calling is for human advancement.

THE ARTS

In the early twentieth century artists like Igor Stravinsky and James Joyce provoked the established world of form and what was critically acceptable as art. They created art forms that mirrored the dissonance of modern life and were initially vilified, and eventually praised, for the freedom of expression their work embodied. Isadora Duncan did for dance what they did for music and literature.

POLITICS AND GOVERNANCE

The suffragettes of the late nineteenth and early twentieth centuries battled the second-class status of women. Later, in the twentieth century, Nelson Mandela provoked the government of oppression so entrenched in South Africa that it would keep him imprisoned on an island for twenty-seven years. I wonder what our present-day equivalent to women not having basic rights is, what condition people in the twenty-second century will look back on with horror and disbelief.

BUSINESS

There are countless stories of *intrapreneurs,* the term coined by consultant and author Gifford Pinchot for innovators in companies who provoke their own management to create anew. Some succeed and their companies gain, but many of these provocateurs lose their employment or leave it in frustration because the soil is too barren for new ideas to take root. Then, they often innovate in another company, or one started by themselves, where they can cultivate the soil to sprout and grow ideas into revenue streams.

SCIENCE

Margaret Mead, early in her career in the 1930s, provoked the field of anthropology to become valuable to the general reading public. She turned science and the pursuit of anthropological truth into popular discussion of cultures and the different ways of being human.

EDUCATION

Maria Montessori left traditional education with its industrial models of turning out children who can pass tests but can't think for themselves. She provoked the educational system to use curriculum designs based on the individual child's gifts for learning as they emerge.

EVERYDAY LIFE

At work, someone on the team won't let her team take a shortcut with a process because it will be at the expense of the customer.

At home, the teenager provokes the rest of the family into discussing how they want to spend their time over the holidays. Do they want to spend all their time shopping for the other members, or do they want to give back to the community in some meaningful way by devoting time to the less fortunate?

A mother initiates a discussion on how to recycle bottles and cans, so the family members have to confront ecological principles and what they do every day to contribute to wastefulness.

I witnessed an everyday provocateur moment a few years ago. A corporate manager, who had begun exploring her spiritual side, decided that she wanted to go to a Buddhist monastery and meditate for a month. Well, she had sort of decided, and was at least talking about it seriously for a time. When she mentioned it to one of my colleagues, an established provocateur, he fired back, "You're a coward if you don't go." Not exactly your standard warm and fuzzy offer of support and praise for having the intention.

After she did go, a few years later, she knew I would see him again and told me to tell him that she had indeed gone to the monastery. "What he said stuck with me," she said, "because he was right."

All provocateurs have one thing in mind, no matter what field they are working in: to wake people up to an injustice and a wrong and to get them beyond their complacency to a place of action.

Here is one story of a provocateur's provocateur, who devoted her life to waking people up. Her life reminds us of the perils and the joys of the provocateur's call.

MARY HARRIS: PROVOCATEUR EXTRAORDINAIRE

In the 1830s in Ireland the Catholics were oppressed by British rule, as they had been with varying degrees of intensity for many centuries. A baby girl born into these conditions would be buried an old lady nearly a hundred years later in middle America, southern Illinois to be exact, having become one of the greatest labor agitators the world had ever seen. One of her early life memories from Ireland in the city of Cork was of British soldiers carrying the severed heads of Irish resisters on pikes through her hometown. The early exposure to violence may have explained why she so often put herself in harm's way in her work decades later—she was born into it.

Her father, Richard Harris, fled to Canada to escape with his life— his father had been hanged as a traitor. The Harris family moved to Chicago, and in her twenties Mary Harris moved to Memphis, where she married George Jones. They lived in a working-class neighborhood and had four children in quick succession. George was a proud member of the Iron Molders' Union, one of the earliest trade unions.

Mary started her family in Memphis, and it ended there as well. When the yellow fever swept through the city, the poor neighborhoods, with people too sick to leave and little health care, were hit the hardest. Mary lost her husband and all four children in the same futile battle with the disease.

She managed to go on, somehow. Six years later she returned to Chicago to become a seamstress, sewing the beautiful dresses of the growing upper class in that city. In 1871, she lost what she had again, this time in the Great Fire. And while returning to a life of labor to make ends meet, Mary's real calling was sparked by the Knights of Labor and the other labor unions that were starting up all over the nation and getting a foothold in the fast industrializing city of Chicago. Mary Harris, listening to the rousing speeches of men like Terrance Powderly, found herself deeply aligned with the causes of labor in the mines and factories to stop child labor and to end the brutally long hours, unsafe conditions, and low wages of the working class.

Now in her forties Mary Harris answered a call to justice in the workplace that would carry her for another fifty years. She started a publication called *Appeal to Reason* in 1895 and in the course of her work took on none other than tycoon John D. Rockefeller. Mary Harris would become the famous and infamous Mother Jones, of course, and she would cross the country for decades, organizing strikes, protests, and generally getting in the face of the industrialists, always pushing for fair treatment.

From our vantage point, if we are middle class or above, it is hard to fathom the working conditions for the men, women, and children getting off the boats and coming off the farms to work in the city's factories or the country's coal mines in the late 1800s.

A common practice in the coal mines was to pay in company scrip rather than dollars. The miners and their families would then have to pay for necessities at the company store, where prices were high. *The result would be miners working sixty-hour weeks for a month, and after receiving pay and using it for rent and food, owing the company money, a kind of negative 401k plan.*

Another abomination that fueled Mother Jones's inner fire was the abuse of children in the factories. In 1895, she observed young children in the cotton mills of Alabama. In her autobiography she wrote, "The children, little children working, the most heartrending spectacle in life. . . . They crawled under machinery to oil it. They replaced spindles all day long, all night long: night through, night through. Tiny babies of six years old with faces of sixty did an eight-hour shift for ten cents a day." Four-year-olds came to the mills to help older brothers and sisters. They, however, received no pay.[2]

Mother Jones showed up at the hottest hot spots of unrest to further her cause. Skilled in attracting publicity, she knew how to get the media to give her cause the coverage she wanted. Unionizing the West Virginia coal mines was a decades-long effort for her. During one of her well-known speeches, in 1912, she held up a mine guard's uniform, full of bullet holes and bloodied, and said it was decorated to suit her. Guns were stockpiled on both sides and Mother Jones would regularly walk into armed territories to hold another rally. Banned from cities and whole states, she would wear disguises and sneak past the guards and police to live in the shanties with "her boys" and their families, as she referred to them.

"If they shoot me, I will talk from the grave," she once told a crowd in Denver.

Ludlow, Colorado, was the scene of her pitched battle with the Rock-efellers, owners of a large mine. With one thousand striking miners and families living in a tent colony, the company guards turned on the strik-ers, torching the tents, firing shots, and using bombs. Twelve children, five men, and two women were killed in the process. Mother Jones tes-tified in Washington after the tragedy, as did John D. Rockefeller, Jr., with whom she later struck up a relationship. "I've licked him many times but now we've made peace," she eventually said.

When Mother Jones died she was most likely in her nineties, although people celebrated her hundredth birthday—May 1, 1930—because no one knew exactly when she was born. By the time she was laid to rest, she and her peers had provoked the country into considering a whole new approach to labor. The major labor legislation of the 1930s owes its existence at least in part to the tireless work of the provocateur from Ire-land whose last five decades of life were a continuous battle against the abuses of the powerful.

At her funeral, one poem read aloud ended with these words:

The wonderful spirit of old Mother Jones
May march up and down
Like the soul of John Brown
Till justice shall vanquish our burdens and groans,
And oppression is buried like old Mother Jones.

WHAT PROVOCATEURS DO

On a dramatic scale Mother Jones illuminates how provocateurs stay true to their calling. While most of us will never do visible work on the scale of a Mother Jones, we can learn from the lessons of the provoca-teurs to battle the issues we do address.

EMBODY THE ISSUES

Provocateurs become the issue, the movement. They live the change needed and they become the hero of those wanting the change and the enemy of those defending the status quo. They become living symbols of what they are fighting for.

Exaggerate to Force Attention

Provocateurs say outlandish and extreme things to make a point and rattle cages. By articulating intense versions of the truth, they crystallize issues, creating an opposite pole from the pole of injustice that exists but few seem willing to see. The freedom marchers in Birmingham in the sixties provoked the response of the bigots, bringing them out of hiding. Exaggerating disobedience to a bad law, rather than quietly ignoring it, allows the provocateurs to create the chemistry for social change.

Martin Luther King is very clear on the subject: "Nonviolent direct action seeks to create such a crisis and establish such creative tension that a community that has constantly refused to negotiate is forced to confront the issue."[3]

Hold Up the Mirror

As a society denies the injustice, the provocateur finds ways to put the wrongdoing in its face. "In case you haven't noticed, society," say the antismoking activists, "there seems to be a connection, in spite of forty years of denial by the companies, between the amount of cool cigarette ads aimed at kids and the amount of lung cancer."

The mirror can be humorous, not grim, as some provocateurs have learned well. In fighting the flat tax idea (which sometimes seems like a good idea given the complexities of tax returns but would disadvantage those who can't afford taxes) the folks in United for a Fair Economy chanted at a rally against the flat tax idea and its former champion, Steve Forbes, with their little rhymes:

"Who needs day care,
Hire an au pair."

"Make workers pay the tax,
So investors can relax."[4]

Pace the Aggravation

Provocateurs know their success depends on timing and applying pressure. Too little pressure, and no change occurs. Too much, and the backlash is so great that the cause is lost. Or worse, the cause is ignored as being hopelessly extreme.

In his lifelong fight against apartheid, Nelson Mandela constantly judged the pace of his activity. He schooled himself in military tactics when he was convinced it was time for destruction of property as a way to cripple the system that was crippling his people.

Formulate Symbols for Communication Nuggets

Provocateurs create the symbols of resistance and energy around which their followers can rally and sustain their energy and focus.

Gifford Pinchot tells a delightful story of an engineer-provocateur bent on innovation who named his innovation project the "Anvil Project." Whenever he wanted to enlist the support of a new person, after the initial meeting he sent them an anvil pin that could fit on a blouse or lapel. The person could wear it proudly, or ignore it, but no one was in the dark as to its blacksmith meaning. The provocateur forged a new method, bending the current process into a new, more usable form. The metaphor stuck (and the project was finished).

In the early days of Ben & Jerry's, Pillsbury was strong-arming distributors not to carry the super-rich ice creams from Vermont. With corporate size and powerful lawyers on Pillsbury's side, the smaller company knew a frontal assault would be useless. So they started an energetic leaflet campaign with the phrase, "What's the doughboy afraid of?" The Pillsbury logo got turned against that firm and the symbol of the doughboy helped draw the matter to a quick close.

From the raised clenched fist of black power in the sixties, to the Greenpeace motorboats scooting in front of the giant whaling boats, to the lone student in Tiananmen Square who blocked the progress of the tank, provoking symbolically is one of the hallmarks of those called to be provocateurs.

GUT IT OUT

Many provocateurs don't see themselves as particularly heroic, but they grow aware of the pain and all the negative consequences that can occur when they buck the system. They are simply willing to absorb the hits for the good of the cause. All callings are about head and heart and guts. This one is strong on the guts part.

Author and consultant Peter Block talks about his more recent work: "The most difficult part [of being called to his current work] is knowing that you are going against the culture. Facing the drowning doubt about practicality. Pursuing efforts that are financially marginal, and having only a small group of people that support them but yourself."

An important attribute of the courage of provocateurs is that it is not a onetime, hero-for-the moment thing. It is a long-term proposition, taking years of fortitude to supply the provocateur with enough stamina for the long haul.

The courage of provocateurs ignites the courage in their peers and followers. It becomes an example to follow, a beacon to light the way. The trail of civil disobedience from Henry David Thoreau to Gandhi to Martin Luther King to César Chavez creates a chain link of courageous acts that send out hope and inspiration for us all.

If they can face jail and death, we ought to be able to face a boss who allows sexual harassment, confront a policy that shrivels instead of enables, or stand up to a teacher who harangues.

GUIDELINES FOR EVERYDAY PROVOCATEURS

Here are some points to keep in mind.

PREPARE FOR ATTACKS AND FIGHT BITTERNESS WITH GOOD HUMOR

As Marcus Aurelius put it:

Today, I shall be meeting with interference, ingratitude, insolence, dis-
loyalty, ill-will, and selfishness . . . [but I] cannot be angry with my
brother or fall foul of him, for he and I were born to work together.

Once the provoking begins, the provocateur has a new, one-uniform
wardrobe: a shirt with a big circle and a bull's eye in the middle of it on
the back. The provocateur becomes a magnet for anger relating to the
issue at hand and many other kinds of anger as well. When you take
your stance, what people don't like about life will be projected onto
you. Much of the anger and criticism won't be deserved as you are
maligned and your motives and intentions are questioned. Unless you
are a contrarian by nature, this will hurt a lot. If you are a contrarian,
it will hurt some eventually anyway.

Be prepared for the injustices and keep an open heart. If you become
bitter, then they have won. If you start to become cynical, do something—forgive your antagonists, read a funny book, go to a movie, eat
some ice cream, take a vacation. Losing your perspective and sense of
humor can be the end of your effectiveness as a provocateur.

PROVOKE THE STIFLERS MORE THAN THEY CAN HANDLE

When those perpetrating the injustice and resisting the change tell you
now is not a good time to provoke and keep pushing, they may be
right. But usually they are not. Your job is to push for the change, confront the system they hold dear, confront them with their own
encrusted habits and faulty beliefs. As their mental models and belief
systems are assaulted, they are the ones who have to deal with their
pain, as best as they know how. That is their job, not yours.

"I have never yet engaged in a direct action that was 'well-timed,'
according to the timetable of those who have not suffered. . . . For
years now I have heard the word 'Wait!'" wrote Martin Luther King,
Jr. in "Letter from Birmingham Jail," one of the bibles for those with
a provocateur's calling.[5]

Don't Become Your Own Myth

It is easy to get righteous about the provocateur's call. After all, aren't you trying to correct an injustice? But the trick is not to mythologize yourself into a heroic battle wherein you embody all virtue and others are the devil incarnate. The status quo may be filled with enemies who think differently from you, but you are lost if you think you are the only source of good on the issue.

One reason provocateurs fail is personalizing the wrongdoing and trying to destroy their enemies instead of their enemies' ideas and practices.

Nelson Mandela gave the perfect example of fighting his own larger-than-life heroic myth, which grew stronger the more years he spent in prison. He invited his captors, the jailers from his Robbin Island life, to his Presidential inauguration. Rather than puffing himself up as the embodiment of all good, he declared that his jailers were good people, victimized as much, if not more, by apartheid than he was, only the mental bars they lived in were not as visible as the physical ones he endured every day.

When you find yourself getting too righteous and self-congratulatory, you are on your way to trouble as a provocateur.

Get Rest and Make Friends

In keeping with the anti-myth rule, provocateurs need to stay rested and make friends along the way. If they aren't careful, when a cause burns in their heart, provocateurs can burn out, approximating the supple texture of something between a strip of crisp bacon and last year's peanut brittle.

Stay loose, provocateurs. Get friends by being one. Take interest in your friends' nonprovocateur but intentional and called lives. Take greater interest in your third-grader's homework. Call your mom and ask her what she is up to. Listen to the oldies and dance on the kitchen floor with your sweetheart.

Burn intensely, provocateurs, and then enjoy a weekend with a mystery novel, Alfred Hitchcock classics, and lots of naps.

BE PREPARED TO ACCEPT DEFEAT

Provocateurs wouldn't be provocateurs if they were working for a sure thing. The call of provocateurs is to work against the odds, to swim upstream, to see the deck is stacked against them and decide to go for it anyway, to put a dent in the problem in some way, knowing that they may never see the result. Others behind them will see the dent and take a swing at it because they did.

That is what provocateurs are called to do—to bear witness to a better way, to a principle that must be remembered when most have forgotten. Provocateurs are ready to lose the round but to stay in the fight, because not to do so would be to sell out to a lower principle, to a wrong that must not be fed.

Peter Block says it best. When he is asked when our social condition will finally improve, when will we see an end to human injustice, when will we turn the corner on the causes that we are working for, he puts it simply:

"It will get better the day after you die."

PROVOKE WHEN YOU HAVE LITTLE AUTHORITY, SPONSOR PROVOCATEURS WHEN YOU HAVE IT

Many a corporate provocateur reports that gray-haired revolutionary roles can be different from the twenty-something and thirty-something versions. Although some gray-hairs stay at it, like Mother Jones, many mellow out with less hormonal support. They grow tired of the energy drain, have kids in college and a mortgage to pay, tolerate less risk, and want to pass on their wisdom. Not only that, somehow they stayed at it long enough, and were lucky or skillful enough, or both, to gain authority. They have become vice presidents of something or other, or their start-up company has become a real place with real jobs. Wasn't Bill Gates part of the revolution a long time ago? Weren't you in a rock band before you woke up and found yourself a director of IT at Acme Services?

It is at this stage in your life that sponsoring provocateurs may well become your calling. Without the seasoned help of a sponsor, many provocateurs run out of resources, or create such a backlash that their idea is snuffed out. Sponsors step in to guide, and generally wise up the provocateurs with their efforts.

Provocateur sponsors are like grandparents, invaluable friends and guides who get to walk away from the direct implementation because the provocateurs need and want to do that part. But a sponsor's calling is not easy. Knowing when to scold, to sooth, to challenge, to protect, to let the provocateur fail miserably if necessary are all part of the many judgment calls sponsors must make.

At a large corporation where I have worked there was a well-known executive who sponsored many a provocateur over the years of his being a senior vice president and eventually president of a six-thousand-person division. He was known for his approachability, his irreverence and outspokenness in the executive suite with his peers, and his protection, tutelage, and ability to squirrel away extra cash in his budget for the provocateur-innovators who needed some to get a project off the ground.

Here are two good resources if you contemplate sponsorship as one of your calls. Gifford Pinchot's *Intrapreneuring: Why You Don't Have to Leave the Corporation to Become an Entrepreneur* written in the ancient 1980s, is a pioneering and classic work that still reads intelligently. His other book, written with Libby Pinchot, *The Intelligent Organization*, is also very helpful and a nineties piece that helps sponsors know what they are sponsoring. And Gary Hamel's *Leading the Revolution*, with unfortunate examples like Enron included (which reminds us what Enron might have been if it stayed value-based and not greed-based), is a fun and insightful read on sponsors as well.[6]

Writer, farmer, ecologist, and teacher Wendell Berry created a poem for us to remember in the times when we may be tempted to take the easy road and miss our summons to be a provocateur.

The Mad Farmer Revolution

Love the quick profit, the annual raise, vacation with pay.
Want more of everything ready made.
Be afraid to know your neighbors and to die.
And you will have a window in your head.
Not even your future will be a mystery any more.
Your mind will be punched in a card and shut away in a little drawer.
When they want you to buy something, they will call you.
When they want you to die for profit, they will let you know.

So, friends, every day do something that won't compute.
Love the Lord.
Love the world.
Work for nothing.
Take all that you have and be poor.
Love someone who does not deserve it.
Denounce the government and embrace the flag.
Hope to live in that free republic for which it stands.
Give your approval to all you cannot understand.
Praise ignorance, for what man has not encountered he has not yet
    destroyed.
Ask the questions that have no answers. Invest in the millenium.
Plant sequoias.
Say that your main crop is the forest that you did not plant, that you
    will not live to harvest.
Say that the leaves are harvested when they have rotted into the mold.
    Call that profit. Prophesy such returns.
Put your faith in the two inches of humus that will build under the
    trees every thousand years.
Listen to carrion—put your ear close, and hear the faint chatterings
    of the songs that are to come.
Expect the end of the world.
Laugh. Laughter is immeasurable.
Be joyful though you have considered all the facts.

So long as women do not go cheap for power, please women more
   than men.
Ask yourself: Will this satisfy a woman satisfied to bear a child?
Will this disturb the sleep of a woman near to giving birth?

Go with your love to the fields. Lie easy in the shade.
Rest your head in her lap. Swear allegiance to what is nighest in your
   thoughts. As soon as the generals and the politicos can predict
   the motions of your mind, lose it.
Leave it as a sign to mark the false trail, the way you didn't go.
Be like the fox who makes more tracks than necessary, some in the
   wrong direction.
Practice Resurrection.[7]

Wendell Berry himself was called—called to remind us that our calls
to living our uniqueness are more likely to come from carrion than
from the newspaper.

(Note for those too young to remember punch cards: If Wendell
Berry were to compose this today and not in the days when IBM punch
cards were the technology of choice, the sixth line, *Your mind will be
punched in a card and shut away in a little drawer, might have read
something like this: Your mind will sit poised in a psychographic database,
ready to be mined.*)

Working for the Destruction of the Negative

Provoke the deconstruction of all conditions that limit human potential, even if you
have no way of knowing what your results will be. From the long history of courageous provocateurs who have lived the courage to make a difference, learn the lessons of what provoking does and how it works.

Be strategic; a provocateur's call is a thinking person's call, one of courage to do the right thing, obviously, but also of strategy to employ well-timed tactics that will work.

At some point, your calling may well be to sponsor other provocateurs by acting as their guide. Be wise in your lessons and guidance.

As the path of courage includes moral alignment and truth, stay true to your conviction without getting holier than thou or bitter. Self-righteous provocateurs are pains in the butt, not to mention a danger to the cause, themselves, and others.

Exercise: Provoking with Skill and Courage

- Think back over your life and see if you have been a provocateur at least a few times. If you are constantly in that mode, are you overdoing it? If you have never confronted an injustice, aren't you being too complacent?
- When did you provoke well, with courage and skill?
- When did you blow it and have poor tactics or courage deficits, or both?
- Have you ever read a book about, or do you have any heroes or sheroes, who are or were provocateurs? If not, why not?
- Does attacking the establishment always turn you off? Why?
- Didn't our founding fathers provoke England? Didn't César Chavez do legitimate work? Do you know a provocateur now who is trying his or her best?
- Isn't there one condition you are aware of where human stifling is the result? How are you working to limit or stop the damage?
- Do you know anyone who needs to be shocked a bit out of complacency?

PART II

Summary

In the course of a lifetime, you will rub up against saboteurs, evocateurs, and provocateurs playing their parts in the world with varying degrees of intensity and skill. Fight off the saboteurs with persistence and learn why they entered your life whenever you can. Wherever you find them, learn the deep lessons from the evocateurs bringing forth your essential gifts and from the provocateurs courageously at work to remove the social limits that strangle those gifts.

You will also find these calls within you, and you will assume the roles that come with them. To put it in its place, starve your inner saboteur, a specialized segment of your ego. But evoke and provoke with all you have to give as the situations of your life require. We express our full humanity and we create better futures when we refuse to leave things as they are, when we stand for nothing less and affirm our truest and highest nature.

PART III

Keeping Focus for the Long Term

In this section we introduce some new concepts while building on some previously introduced, all in the spirit of helping us, with both practical tips and inspiration, to sustain our callings over long life spans. In chapter 7 we pick up the theme of the ego and its challenges, taking it beyond the inner saboteur that was discussed earlier. Unfortunately, the ego is much more complex and does far more than just act as saboteur on occasion. It can create multiple diversions from your call.

We return to the evocateur in the last chapter to help us reconsider some of the issues that arise as callings are lived over time, through routines and everyday roles. And we wrap up the discussion by listening to our colleagues on their paths.

Go Gently Against the Ego 7

HERE'S THE GROUND we've covered so far:

- Believing in your calling is the only insurance that you'll have one.
- Building a portfolio of calls is the means to be conscious and do well in multiple life roles.
- Fighting off saboteurs strengthens your response to a calling.
- Evoking the possibilities of the moment is fundamental.
- Provoking the status quo to change is the calling when conditions are stifling.

Now we need to look at the frequent and fundamental challenges we face as we answer any of the calls we discern. The questions we address in this chapter are these:

- How can I be sure my ego is not interfering with my responses to a sound calling by providing false messages?

■ How do I address the fears that can paralyze or distort my efforts to live out a called life?

■ Responding to a call is strenuous. Where is the fun in all this?

MANAGING FALSE MESSAGES

One of the more constant challenges is learning to discern the difference between a real calling and the high-sounding impostor calls that divert us from our true paths.

Although answering a call means moving beyond the social messages external to us, there is another force that needs to be addressed for a calling to become a lived reality, an inner force. It is most commonly referred to as the *ego*.

The ego, as different from personality and self, needs some explanation. Up to this point I have used the term to refer to that side of us that might get in the way of a calling. Since we are going deeper here into the issues of the ego, I'll define what I mean in layman's terms, contrasting it with self and personality.

Personality is the container, the outer shell for our egos and our selves. It is the way we think and feel, and it can be measured through psychological tests and observed in everyday encounters. When someone at a party says, "I am an ENFP"—the shorthand from the Myers-Briggs instrument that has become a code for so many—that person is engaging in the near-ubiquitous language of personality typing. Whether you think creatively or analytically, what you find interesting or funny, whether your feelings are spontaneous or measured—all are in the realm of personality.

Self is the higher will in action, the transcendent part of you connected to others and the universe that drives you to authenticity and adding value in the world. It is the seat of your highest aspirations, your soul.

Ego lies between personality and self. Personality is inherited and conditioned, ego is both inherited and conditioned and it is formed by our will. Ego is the personality tied to the lower will, the part containing the drives for security, power, pleasure, competition, and survival. One of the ego's biggest jobs is the construction of life roles out of these drives so that we can get our needs met while also being productive members of society.

In normal conversations with others we often are operating from personality and ego rather than self. How the day went, what happened at work, how the team is doing—this is not the deeper stuff of our lives. This is the news of our days. Self-level topics are purpose, values, and principles that operate at the level of being. And of course, calls and callings and vocations are self- and soul-talk.

The ego operates at a different level of our being than the self, and it is helpful because it defines us and gives us energy and motivation to survive and thrive. It assesses our talents and helps us launch careers. It serves a useful function, assembling a life, our ego structure, carrying us into careers and marriages and roles that help us succeed.

Angels, as far as we know, don't have egos; they are pure essence and don't need roles. (For those of you who don't believe in angels, take this metaphorically.) But for us incarnate folk, the ego, and the collection of roles it attaches itself to, constitute how we live in the world—activist, parent, barbecue hobbyist, marketer—and give form to our lives. The positive use of the ego attaches us to the roles and responsibilities that become our lives (unless of course a person chooses a negative role for the ego, like a computer virus designer, but few such people have purchased this book).

Positive functions aside, even the best-inclined egos pose challenges. They will taint even your most noble thoughts with their own concerns.

I heard an accomplished spiritual teacher on a lecture tour once joke, as he was preparing himself for his presentation on compassion, "Knowing how many seats we have sold is one of the bigger parts of my preparation."

If you dislike the ego because it gets in the way of your higher self and gives voice to some of the less noble parts of your being, you are in trouble, but you are not alone. None of us enjoys grappling with this part of our being, but the troubling part is that the ego is here to stay.

Unless you lock yourself away to pray in a convent, monastery, or ashram for twenty years, your ego is not about to disappear. The reports from those who have tried this lock-yourself-away approach agree that the ego survives intact anyway. The ego is impossible to snuff out, or ignore, even though both methods are often tried by those passionate about their calling and who have a spiritual sense of what they are about. The attempt to eliminate the ego is understandable because it can take you down the wrong path so easily, but it is futile.

In fact, attempts to eliminate it only make the ego stronger and harder to work with.

(On the polar side of snuffing out the ego, there are the legions who are not interested in callings and let their egos have at it. Living from their surface, and defining themselves by their ego status and accomplishments, this is all they know. These folks aren't reading this book either, unless a devoted or frustrated spouse has put them up to it—or they are thinking about giving up the computer virus business.)

The ego is fueled by ever-active hormonal-biological drives, and with all its needs for status and power and pleasure it is a force that anyone who wants to answer a calling has to contend with. With the ego acting as the inner force that colludes with the ever-present social messages to stay shallow, we often wander off the paths to which our calls summon us.

Since the ego is never going to go away, people answering their calls need to learn to combat it skillfully, lest the ego muffles or distorts the calling to a life of significance and service.

How to contend with, direct, and even be in flow with the ego is worth discussing for all those who are responding to a call, fighting off their own inner saboteur, or provoking the destruction of an evil.

We will look at three methods to do so: accepting positive fear, maintaining your sense of humor, and cooperating with the ego and its drives when possible.

But first let's look at a few of the ego's favorite tricks and ploys.

THE EGO IN DISGUISE

Our egos devise ways of disguising themselves as legitimate voices from the self to guide us on our way. The great classic on this from twentieth-century literature is *The Screwtape Letters* by C. S. Lewis.[1] If you haven't read this, buy the book and learn about the ego at work, told in the metaphor of a pesky, minor devil attempting to get people to turn away from service and concern for the whole by whispering rationalizations in their ears as if they were their own best thoughts.

Here are samples of the ego at work:

What a person with a call to leadership might hear: "The community needs a leader and it seems that I am here to respond to this need. Getting elected with a few hidden promises to supporters is just the way these positions are secured."

What a person with a call to her profession might encounter: "This is the perfect career move. The family won't mind if I add just a little more to my workday. There is no question this offer is my ship coming in."

What people called to family will tell themselves: "I really need this raise for our security, which is what my family needs. I know I won't like the work nearly as much, but for the family, I gotta do it."

What a man called to the marketplace might encounter: "I need to assert my power for the good of my product line. Our mission demands that I take a visible position here. I will forget about the team for the time being. . . . I can get back to that later."

What a woman called to both the marketplace and the family might fool herself with: "It would be good to establish myself with him as someone he can trust, so we should probably take this business trip together—but let's not tell our spouses, why worry them? They wouldn't understand how we can handle this complex relationship."

None of these ego-voices is a ticket to call-obliteration by themselves. They are normal. But when we get sloppy and the outcome is workaholism, an affair, a meaningless title, an unneeded raise at the expense of quality family time, too much power, or anything else that taints our motives and inflates a role beyond its positive aspects, the soul feels the price. The price is a lack of alignment between the soul's direction and the energies of the psyche. You experience inner dissonance. You end up going in two directions at once, and the greater the ego deception the greater the dissonance.

A GRAND CAPACITY FOR FIBBING

The ego has more ploys than merely disguising itself—it can muffle the dissonance and numb our brains and beings to the suffering and anxiety of being internally misaligned. The ego pulls this off through mental and emotional tricks. Two of the more common tricks are rationalization and getting busy with diversions. With skillful numbing methods—in most of us an advanced ego capacity—the defense mechanisms shut down the feedback of the incongruity within the self as long as possible, and the price it carries.

For many of us, even with a lot of effort at fooling ourselves, ignoring the dissonance and the rationalizations of the ego is an arrangement that is doomed. But for some, this effort can last a lifetime. Psychologist Alfred Adler gave this long-term capacity to fool ourselves a great and telling name: *the life lie.*

***

Often we meet people with large amounts of personal power and ego strength, living large with positions and influence, and they are living a life lie, not in touch with the self or attending to calls, and perhaps they never will.

***

Our culture's current attraction to celebrities from every walk of life feeds this life lie phenomenon. The accoutrements of a big car, an impressive job title, and the right social circle can make the life lie feel pretty good. The ego makes us think we are our own little celebrities.

The ego game usually runs its course, however. Not always, but usually, because almost all of us get bored or feel empty or get fired or lose a loved one, and the deeper side of life shows up, and the pain of not living out our larger side begins to be felt.

Unmasking the Ego: Exposing the Lie

After a time—sometimes a long time—of the ego having its say and using various maneuvers and tricks, most of us allow our real voice to show up and do battle with those misguided rationalizations. Our callings from the level of self take on our egos. Our higher selves confront our lower selves.

Self: Hey, let's talk about the hours you are keeping at work—a little much, don't you think?

Ego voice: Naw! I barely put in the minimum for someone at my level.

Self: Can we have a chat about your executive friend, the one you want to take another trip with?

Ego voice: Why do we need to talk about him? It is purely a business friendship and we get a lot of work done for the company.

And so the ego and the self duke it out for a person's energy and decisions, one wanting to continue the numbing and the scam and the other counting on the long-term need for inner alignment with callings, principles, and self-expression. The numbing is important for the preservation of the ego because without it the feedback from the self is overwhelming, the dissonance grows intolerable, and the call comes screaming through in the form of a magnificent obsession to live with integrity. Numbing with a little alcohol, or with friends who encourage the self-deception—"A little gambling never hurt anybody, even if it is daily"—or with any of its various tools and forms, buy the ego a little more time to play its game and put off attention to our calls.

With reflection and being honest with ourselves, we grow more skillful in telling the real calls from the imitations.

With practice and judgment, we figure out how the ego's inauthentic messages get us into, instead of out of, danger, and take us off our path instead of showing us the way.

We make mistakes along the way, of course. The judgment we develop is often a direct corollary to how many difficult spots we got ourselves and others into as we pursued the imitation messages to their troublesome and bitter ends. And for this we have to forgive ourselves. The trick is to facilitate the dialogue between ego and self as soon as possible, as often as it is needed, so we don't mistake the silly ego replacements for our real life. The errors we make earlier in life are often mistakes of a lack of consciousness—not knowing the difference between our lower selves and higher selves or the difference between a slick rationalization and a calling. The mistakes we make later in life, after we have had time to become more discerning, though still forgivable, are less so, because they are less about discernment and more about courage.

The Ego-Self Dialogue

Susan (not her real name) has been poised in a polished career and motherhood for two decades. But a recent divorce and the staleness of the career have clearly signaled that her life needs to shift to one that is less involved with career management and expected motherhood roles (the kids are nearly grown) and more about calls and responses to the heart.

Over this several-year coaching relationship I have admired Susan's logic and patience. As she has had sudden heart rushes to move into new work territory, to move physically out of a small college town, and to explore who she might be when she is not just playing her old roles well, she ponders, using the logic that has and will continue to serve her and more of her feelings as well. "How should I approach these decisions?" she asks, more of herself than of me. I have been more of a mirror than adviser. My role has been to encourage Susan's ego-self dialogue, in effect complicating her process a bit, so she gets used to challenging what would have been formerly easy answers supplied by her history, her successes, her ego. "These feelings to move on are surprising me in their strength and timing. I am not ready yet, or I don't think I am," she says with some doubt and hope for the new feelings.

Susan senses the good that her ego structure and drives have done for her over the years, and the limits to using all the same inner methods now that she faces a crossroads. If she allows herself and musters up the courage, I will bet she has a more called life in front of her, one that she somehow senses and will allow to emerge, in its own time.

LEANING INTO FEAR

One sign that the real voice, the substantive call, is at work is feeling a kind of fear. If the voice makes you quake a bit, or even a lot, on the big issues you face, then you may well be on the right path. When it comes to fear, however, positive fear needs to be distinguished from ego fear.

Voice-driven fear is not the adrenaline rush you feel before getting on a roller coaster, although that surely has its place. Your average bank robbers—and haven't we all known a few—feel fear as they put on the nylon-stocking masks. This is not the fear we are talking about. (Picture a professional thief on trial whose self-defense goes as follows: "Your honor, with all due respect, you must allow for the fact that some of us are called to do unusual work. Since I was twelve I knew it was my unique gift and my special duty to take other people's deposits at financial institutions and use them for my good. In this way, I have accepted the burden of becoming a master of resource redistribution. It is my calling.")

Positive fear when it comes to callings is not of the cheap-thrill variety, nor about any of the ego anxieties of the lower order. These kinds of fear show up when we think we are likely to lose status or some pleasure we have enjoyed. These kinds of fear are of the "What-will-they-think-of-me?" "What-if-I-am-having-a-bad-hair-day?" and "Oh, no, if-I-serve-on-that-board-I-won't-have-time-for-my-sitcom-reruns" variety.

Conversely, fear in the face of a calling is about a duty, a need to do something that is not easy, that you may or may not love or be totally equipped for, and which you know will both put something into you and take something out of you.

The fear of the call is a soulquake, a being-tremor as a life challenge that is worthy of you and reveals itself to your deepest place of being. This is the fear that requires moral courage as its response.

The Kierkegaard phrase "fear and trembling," which I mentioned in the first chapter of the book, captures these moments of soul-dread in living life head-on. The term is true enough to many people's experience.

Nor does the trembling go away when we want it to, or fade into the woodwork when we get older. Listen to Steve Sheppard's view of this anxiety:

> *I question the propriety of the call [as CEO] constantly. I doubt I will ever know with absolute certainty that this was the right direction, the right vocation, the right use of my abilities. . . . To the extent that I "survive" this ongoing scrutiny, I affirm the directions I've chosen for myself. But at the end of my career, I still expect to be asking the questions that surface at the end of the movie* Saving Private Ryan. *The older Ryan asks, "Have I led a good life? Have I been a good man?" The asking of the question is maybe as valuable as the various answers that I give along the way.*

The soulquake stems from the fact that when the true call makes itself heard through the noise of the social messages and the chatter of the ego, it is quite different from what we thought it would be, so different that we don't know if we can handle it. The call challenges the safety we enjoy in our current world. The call can be far removed from the life we thought we deserved and to which we thought we were progressing.

It could go something like this:

"I thought I was supposed to be the vice president of discontinued products at All-World Enterprises in Tucson. Instead, it feels like I am being called to be the branch manager at Acme Email Enterprises. What kind of a dismal joke is this?"

Acme is in Keokuk. It is one-tenth the size of company you thought you needed. You manage fewer people and have zero perks and a title of branch manager. At Acme you fear the death of your career, a shriveling of your future, a loss of the obvious status to which you are entitled. You sense you are going nowhere and missing your big chance, that you will waste your talent in a little corner of the world, at an unexciting company, one not worthy of you.

But when you allow yourself to look at the Acme-Keokuk package for what it is, when you listen to the call without the ego's fears, distortions, and false demands, it has the right company culture and mission and team, in a good city for your family, and it fits your profile of where you can add value and make a difference.

The inner debate is about the ego needing to support its inflated expectations (Tucson and All-World Enterprises) supported by the social messages, or peer or spousal or parental pressure, and your real self wanting to make your called life happen. You progress in your calling by squelching your ego need; you swallow hard and realize that your ego is not the only source of advice or feedback. Your true self insists, appearances to the contrary, that something, many things, are very right about Acme and the rolling farmland of Iowa, and you say yes to the branch manager job.

The call is often like that—putting you in places you had no idea you'd end up, giving you the situations your soul prescribes, not the ones your ego wanted.

You make the decision in "fear and trembling," mustering up the courage to choose the soul-based option. You are summoned and you know it. Somehow you know that more lasting, infinite-connected work waits for you in Keokuk, and you know you need to attach yourself to it. You deserved Tucson and All-World, and that isn't the point. You'll serve yourself and the world better in Keokuk.

But you are free.

You can always blow it, and go to Tucson and let the ego have its way. In which case, you'll have to dig out of the mess that it will make, or the boredom you will feel, or many of the other symptoms that ego-based choices eventually bring down on your head.

Another indication that the real voice and not your ego is at work is when the cause or the problem you address is beyond what you could possibly finish in your lifetime with even your most Herculean efforts. When you work for ten years eliminating poverty and there are more poor people in the world than when you started, you have a calling. When you work toward perfection in composing uplifting music, when you strive to be a model of service every day, you align yourself with a cause and you have a calling without limits.

Egos can set large goals for sure, but often they set attainable ones so the ego can gloat. Like the athlete making a big play on the field and then prancing around for the fans, a goal achieved is a rush of the first order. But calls, while offering the joy of progress on many occasions, ultimately attach you to causes so infinite, ideals so pure, that to attain them is not possible. You live in service of the call and its principles, not to somehow attain them.

These commitments to calls help you realize how much more significant the calling is than your efforts. What you alone can accomplish in the confines of how long you live and breath on the third planet from the sun takes its proper place alongside the expansiveness of the call.

Paradoxically, the call enlarges you because it is your vehicle for emerging out of your little life span and its limits, and it simultaneously dwarfs you because it is so much bigger than you.

Reinhold Niebuhr captured this ego-escaping element of the call when he said:

Nothing that is worth doing can be achieved in our lifetime; therefore we must be saved by hope.

Nothing which is true or beautiful or good makes complete sense in any immediate context of history, therefore we must be saved by faith.

Nothing we do, however virtuous, can be accomplished alone; therefore we must be saved by love.[2]

Calls are large enough to invite others, sometimes many others, along with us to their ends, and to take us past our futures, the absurdities of our time, and our limited sense of our abilities.

THE FUN FACTOR

In all matters relating to answering the call and gently or firmly negating the impact of our egos, we are more effective if we keep a sense of humor. There may be deep-down apprehension about these matters, but there are also some kicks, some yuks, some belly laughs and joys.

One indicator that a call is an impostor coming from the ego and not the true self is the self-importance you may feel. If a person takes on airs of "I'm on a mission and isn't it good that I am doing this," that person is in trouble because he is off the track. Although the call itself may be noble and true, the response is ego-tainted. Such people will generally suffer setbacks and pain until they can get their inflated egos under better control.

Beware of people with stained-glass tones in their voices, and especially yourself. This often happens in the early stages of responding to the inner voice, when the lasting quality of the call and its grandness naturally tends to pump up the ego.

The George Bernard Shaw quote shown at the beginning of the chapter—"The true joy in life is being used for a purpose recognized by yourself as a mighty one, the being a force of nature"—speaks to the grandness of the call.

With such powerfully formed, even rousing, language it is sometimes difficult to keep a sense of humor about it all—after all, what a person is called to can be very important, and at the least it has lasting value.

But it is precisely the importance of the call that generates the humor—look who's responding to the call to live out these huge causes, it is us. Some of us are smart and talented, and bent on good, surely, but even with all our efforts over generations, we haven't managed to make much of a dent in evil, or universal health, or violence, or a few hundred other huge human and life conditions. And with the advances of modern living we can now blow up or poison the planet.

Jerry Garcia said it best in his Grateful Dead tone: "Somebody has to do something, and it is incredibly pathetic that it has to be us."

Once when I was working with a management team at a large hospital, it occurred to the team how enormous the problems are that humanity faces. They were teetering on the immobility that comes with immensity—the what-difference-can-we-really-make problem. My co-worker went with the direction of their thoughts to make them confront their hope: "That's right, you only have influence over two thousand employees and several hundred patients and their families in any given month. Just our city alone has almost two million people. That is a ridiculously small impact to have on this area, don't you think?"

Everyone laughed at the irony of the paradoxical true-untrue element of the statement. And after the laugh, the humor, the fun, they went back to work. They had a work calling—they were in health care to serve.

Answering a call is far too important to take seriously.

Cooperating with the Ego

Since the ego won't go away, part of the work of answering a call is to put the ego and its considerable energy in service of the call and your higher life causes whenever you can. Going gently, not strenuously, against the ego is an advanced strategy for responding to calls. Shut down the ego only when you really have to, when it is obvious it is taking you down the wrong path.

Really beautiful, really smart, really powerful people have a big job here. Beauty, intelligence, and power are so rewarded in the world that some gifted with any of the three or a combination build grand ego success. Then they get trapped in that success and live on ego, not soul energies. Tragic celebrity stories are fodder for legends here. Elvis and Marilyn and countless others are mythic examples of those with such outlandish ego success that making the transformation to a call-based life seems to have been impossible for them.

But we cannot reject our careers, our beauty and talent, our sexual energy to engage others, or our drive to achieve and win. Quite the opposite. In fact, we must pursue them with intensity and see where our gifts take us, keeping in mind that we are called beyond worldly results.

You'll need to know when you are addicted to the achievements, the power, the thrills and chills of sexual attraction, the money and the accolades. When the addictions and dissatisfactions set in, then it is time to let the callings show up and the self take over. And this can take a while, a long while, during which time you will feel confused and as if you are slipping. The ego made it so easy, and now it seems so hard.

Whereas Elvis and Marilyn are counterexamples, consider the positive examples you know of successful people who have made the transition to a called life. Jimmy Carter works on behalf of the planet. Some rich people become philanthropists of the highest sort. Movie stars and rock stars find causes—some more successfully than others, of course. If a former president and rock stars can use their ego energy and the place they have achieved in the world for more call-based work, so can we all.

The work of fueling your response to your calls includes harnessing your large reserves of ego energy when they can be so directed, of sublimating them to your higher life causes.

Knowing when to put the soul in charge, with its clear or unclear grasp of its calls, and when to use the competitive and winning and juicy drives of the ego at work, is part of the wisdom to develop in making your calls work.

Expect mistakes, learn, and move on.

The Midnight Voice as the Ego and Self Duke It Out

Pssssst. . . .

Pause. . . . I roll over and fluff my pillow.

Pssssssssst, John.

On the second *Pssst,* I usually hear it, and then go back over the last few seconds in my mind and realize that I heard the first Pssst, but didn't really want to.

It is often late when I hear this voice, in the wee hours as I go to bed, but not always. It may come to me on a walk, as I putter in the garden, walking across a parking lot on my way to an appointment.

I wonder sometimes what the origin of the voice is.

I have more spiritual interpretations that are possible, but I usually settle for a simple one: it's me talking to me about the important things. What it definitely is not is the normal inner head chatter of the "Do-I-want-a-latte-today?" variety. I hear this chattering voice inside my head all day as I read, try to listen in countless work discussions, have thoughts that come and go, and email my tush off.

It is this one certain voice, however, rising above the inner chatter and often coming at quite unexpected times, that gets my attention, because this voice is about the big decisions, the issues that are at the root of my integrity.

John, what do you think you are doing pursuing that project with the universities? Do you really think that is going to add value, or do you just want to get the credentials so it looks good and makes you feel a little more important?

At times I get annoyed with these questions from the voice inside my head. If I am tired, if it's in the wee hours when the voice shows up, I want to brush it off.

Can't we talk later, like when I have some energy and am not so busy and in need of sleep?

This response usually has some truth to it, but in most instances it is an elegant denial and kind of procrastination that sounds very reasonable, satisfying my integrity needs. But it is an avoidance ploy just the same.

No, not later, says the voice. *We have got to talk now. Just what do you think you are doing?*

I've learned to join in on the dialogue at this point. This is often the essence of the call in the little matters in my life that, when viewed over time, make up the essence of how I answer the call overall, in the biggest sense of my life. It is in many of these little matters that the call happens or doesn't, gets refined or squelched, sparks and eventually comes shining through or grows dull and tarnished.

Well, what do you think I am doing? I'm talking to the universities so our customers will have another option. The credentials are what we need for them—this isn't about my ego. I don't think.

Well, maybe it is a little bit, but . . .

And so it goes. At times the voice has some ego-trimming to do.

Actually, the ego-trimming is quite frequent. . . .

OK, I can't remember a time when it didn't happen.

I ignore this voice at my own peril.

Teaching the Self and the Ego to Collaborate

One of the more predictable dilemmas of living with a call is the battle with the ego. Strong and clever, useful and very destructive, the ego is loaded with energies we can both use and stem: use them when they can be put in service to a call, and stem them when they gobble us up in frivolity and vanity.

Learning the ego ploys of disguise and numbing is the place to begin. You will educate yourself on which weaknesses of your being and mind your ego can manipulate as you make mistakes in trying to discern and live your calls.

Positive fear and some humor will help you on your way to combating ego messages. Using your ego when you can is a way to avoid pretending you don't have one and are a pure, called person.

There is no such thing as an ego-less life. There is only ego and self and the work of discernment we all face when our calls show up in our lives.

EXERCISE: REFLECTING ON EGO CONTAINMENT

- What are some of the more advanced tactics your ego uses to assert itself in your life? Appeals to pride? Laziness or complacency? Not allowing you to see your self-serving motives?
- How do you best combat and contain your ego?
- How can you use the considerable energy your ego provides to put that energy into the service of your calls?

  Can your competitiveness be used for customers, for coaching kids?

  Can your pride be transmuted into a drive for high quality?

  Can your fears motivate you to service?

  Can you use your need to look good to help others be at their best?

- What successes from your past—like a career with momentum, for example—can you build upon to surrender to the different kind of success your callings bring?

Work the Veil ⑧

I KNOW I AM ANSWERING MY CALL WHEN I HAVE TREMENDOUS ENERGY,
WHEN I AM IN FLOW, WHEN I HAVE THIS CHEESY GRIN MOST OF THE TIME
AND WHEN THINGS JUST WORK. IF I CAN'T GET SOMETHING DONE,
SOMEHOW IT JUST WASN'T NECESSARY.

Sandy Smith
Consultant and coach, Seattle

ACCEPTING MY LIMITATION AND WEAKNESSES WAS PART
OF GETTING BETTER AT MY CALLING.

Donna Ryan
Program Coordinator, Kansas City Downtown Cathedral

WE HAVE COME A LONG WAY, have reached the last chapter, but I hope you still have questions. I know I do. The more I work with callings the more questions I have. Although we have covered substantial ground there is more to cover than any one book, or even many books, can handle. We are talking about life after all, not computer code.

As we conclude in this chapter, we return to some of the basics and to the questions that never go away completely:

- How can I tap the deeper currents that make life worth living for myself and others?
- How can I make my everyday life a more call-based experience?
- How can I keep my perspective on my calling, neither being dwarfed by its scale nor swept up in its grander dimensions?

To address these questions we will return to the mindset and soulset of the evocateurs, which we began to explore in chapter 5. And we will hear from people who were interviewed for this book, many of whom you have already heard from at least once. They have more important insights and gems to add.

EVOCATEURS REVISITED

Answering your call every day takes an attitude and some practice.

The attitude is the one we discussed early on: you have to believe mightily that you have a life summons to evoke the latent potential in yourself and others. The practice of seeing latent possibilities and affirming them develops the mental habits by which all of us called to be evocateurs of everyday life can live.

Some decades ago, as I observed myself and others in teaching and coaching situations, I noticed the phenomenon of people mentally escaping their current reality and going to another realm. They would leave the here-and-now, the seminar room or the classroom we were in, and take an imaginary journey to the world described in a story the teacher was telling, or the world of the video they were watching, or the case we were exploring.

The mind has an innate capacity to shift from the world of its current surroundings to the world of the person who is speaking, to shift rapidly to world after world in rapid succession, all in the imagination. And I observed how this happened in all kinds of settings, not just the formal teaching environment. It is part of how we converse and communicate.

In our minds, there is a very thin veil between these worlds. A psychiatrist once told me that the distance between what people see and feel in the now is a "psychic millimeter" from what they can imagine. A thin veil indeed.

As I worked with teachers and students and leaders and teams, the best of them could traverse those psychic millimeters quickly and effectively, helping people sense what their possibilities were. When I first started giving seminars, lots of them, in my thirties, I would watch participants dive into their deepest imagination. I gave this capability of getting others to sense other realities a name: working the veil. Evocateurs work the veil regularly, not for escapism or to impress others, but to help people leave the constraints of this dimension, get out of normal mind to more creative mental space, in order to see where they might go next.

Here are three practices to help you develop the evocateur's gift. The ability to work the veil is a fundamental mental and emotional skill for living a long-term called life.

LOOK UNDERNEATH THE BEHAVIOR TO THE SPIRIT AND INTENTION

Look past the behavior that your physical eyes can see to the spirit that lies behind it. This develops your mental eyes, your ego-self double-focus vision—one focus on the real and one on the potential.

Don't be literal. Accept nothing at face value. Always assume something deeper is going on.

The natural tendency to look past behavior is something we all have, but in most people it stays underdeveloped.

If a teenager starts to smoke, the parent sees the behavior and searches past it for motive and spirit; the adolescent has a raging desire to belong to her peer group and smoking is in.

If a husband gets crankier than normal, his wife, in her better moments, will assume the attacks are not personal. She'll go underneath the behavior to see the fatigue or anxiety that is causing it.

Tommye Wealand, one of those interviewed for this book, said this in her response to my survey question on what it is like to have a calling. She describes this act of looking past the behavior as central to her purpose in work and life: "Because people are important to me, *I will strive to look for their positive side and to look past what may just lie on the surface.* . . . I will help others reach *their* goals" (italics hers).

This unnatural tendency to see more than meets the eye is what practiced evocateurs working from the self and not the ego expand into a natural act. They view the world constantly for its potential, not just its reality.

ASSUME THE YEARNING

The promises of the enormous advertising machine in our consuming society, the hopes the politicians put out as their product, the invitations of religious leaders to live a better life—these don't exist by accident. Yearning for more and better, for beautiful and lasting, for pain-free and pleasure, for peace and joy, for God and love—this yearning is universal and intense.

Some yearning is more like craving. When that is the case, the ego is in charge. Some yearning is self-based and heart-centered, and as such, is the stuff of our souls. Knowing which is which takes time, reflection, and maturity.

People who are responding to a call watch everyday behavior at work and in families and communities and they see the yearning that drives the behavior, the longing in the heart that only responding to calls can assuage.

Practice seeing what others yearn and search for in their need to get on with a life of meaning. They may be combining their soul journey with all kinds of ego-contaminated cravings, but you needn't give up on them in their longing, whether it is hidden or exposed, pure or polluted.

Assume that everyone yearns. Scratch a person on the surface, even someone who is all crusted up in stale attitudes and ego entanglements, and you will find a soul beneath, one ready to grow, if only invited in a way that person can hear.

Let's look at a few earlier examples. Coach Robey worked the veil when he saw a teachable moment, knew I was ready for some input, and declared me a shooter. To use a sublime example, Martin Luther King's entire "I Have a Dream" speech was a masterpiece of working the veil as he painted the picture of what we could become with lasting racial harmony. He assumed the yearning all people of all colors have for lives of justice and peace.

Those answering a call among us assume the yearning. They give it direction. They find and work the veil because they stay in the calling zone.

FRAME PEOPLE'S ACTIONS IN MEANING-STEEPED MOTIVES

From the beginning, I have asserted that this book is intended more for the person whose calling isn't always obvious than for the superstars who have an obvious and visible calling. The work of callings often falls upon the less-than-obvious, looking-for-the-lost-envelope (that is, Kierkegaard's envelope) crowd. The roles we assume in life aren't always steeped in purpose. Roles are transformed into callings only when we make them so, often with an evocateur or two helping us attain the right mindset.

A full-time parent washing clothes, driving kids to events, and putting meals together can feel less than ennobled by the mundane chores. A business executive can get lost in the repetition of meeting customers and meeting budgets. A craftsman in a building or one more house not very much different than the last one can find the routine overwhelming the craft. The veil is indeed very thin between the uninspiring tyranny of routine and inspiring acts of routine work and duty by those called to see their significance.

The deeper calling in all human roles stems from combined acts of human will and surrender that make these mundane chores rich with meaning and intensely valuable.

The parent who's answering his call sees the routine chores as a means to serve his children and shape their souls.

The business leader answers the call by living the company's values: growing its profits by growing its people and adding to the quality of life of its customers.

Tradespeople do it by seeing their work as a personal expression of lasting value.

In living our calls, we line up with the deepest possibilities behind the veil of routine chores. We must never let go of the meaningful substrate lying beneath the surface of our daily activities. Rooted in the subscript of meaning and purpose, the evocateur in us shows up to do our calling work when others live only by the script.

Those working in kairotic time declare hidden meanings and create their response to their common calls when others are caught in the literal and superficial. They evoke the potential of deeper hopes and meaning by acknowledging that the meaning is always there, but for the will of the doer of the task, of the person behind the role, of the self behind the ego.

By working the veil, the thin boundary between what is and what can be, the evocateur in each of us brings new options and hope to the world. We all work the veil whenever we imagine something that could be better. Evocateurs work the veil with skill, intention, and timing for the lasting positive development of us all.

A SANDWICH DREAM-WEAVER

Some years ago, while working as a customer service consultant for a large hospital, I became very well acquainted with many on the management staff. One of the senior vice presidents was particularly passionate about creating positive moments and experiences throughout the hospital for patients and their families, and he grew greatly concerned about how poor the food service was in the cafeteria. The problem with the food was that it was institutional and the problem with the service was that it was impersonal and almost nonexistent.

After having been away for a few weeks I returned for a meeting with the vice president. At the end of the meeting he announced: "Hey, let's go to lunch in the cafeteria. You've got to see Arnold at work."

As we walked the long, convoluted hallways on the way to the cafeteria, the VP told me that Arnold was a new cafeteria employee who had suggested a sandwich line at lunchtime and that he was making a big impact on the service.

So I got in line and waited my turn to see what Arnold was up to. When I got close enough I could hear the chatter with each customer and the fun that Arnold was having with everyone who craved a sandwich for lunch.

It was my turn.

"Hello," said a smiling Arnold. "What can I get for you today? Your first time here, correct?" Arnold had a standard opening but apparently remembered his customers.

"Yup, first time," I said. "How about turkey on whole wheat?"

"Coming right up," said Arnold. "And may I make a few recommendations on the condiments and trimmings?"

The organizational consultant had met a sandwich consultant.

"Uh, sure, uh, what do you think?"

"Well, there's several ways we could go here," sandwich expert Arnold continued, and while he cut and compressed and put on the condiments and all, he gave me several tips and told me how the next time, oil and some different cheese would create a whole new gustatory event for me.

Then came his signature moment.

Arnold had been to a Japanese steakhouse or something like it. Rather than the normal slice of the sandwich in two, he grabbed his kabuki knife, and cocking it back like a Frisbee on a sidearm throw, made an exaggerated slicing motion that cut my unique turkey creation into perfect halves on its little plate.

Arnold had quite the flair.

He handed me the sandwich and I remember thinking it was more like a lovewich. I wondered if I should somehow store it rather than eat it. I said thanks and Arnold's good-bye smile to me was his greeting smile for the next customer.

Arnold had worked the veil. I felt engaged and charmed, humored and delighted. It was a great sandwich. It was an even better human encounter.

The vice president was right. Arnold indeed had made a difference. So much so that they promoted him to shift supervisor of the servers. I thought management had blown it and Peter-principled him to the wrong level. Arnold, however, had this gift of having all of him show up as a supervisor too.

He had inherited some rather uninspired shift workers as team-mates—"dim bulbs," as one of the managers referred to them—ones who mainly threw the food onto the shelves and did little else. Arnold tried to get them to meet the customers with a little charm and appropriate engagement, but he faced some indifference and initial resistance. When I walked through the cafeteria about a month later, however, I noticed that all the workers were more engaging and warm.

I asked how Arnold had inspired the changes.

"Well, we aren't sure of everything he has done," said the VP, rather bursting with pride and enjoying the cafeteria that Arnold was transforming, "but we do know this. His people weren't getting it so he put out cue cards with these different greetings at the food stations, hidden from the customer but visible to the server, and he apparently changes them often and then recognizes the servers who are the most friendly and creative.

"Whatever he is doing, he's got it going."

I returned for several months, during all of which time the servers had it going under Arnold's leadership (although the sandwich line was not as much fun without him).

Who knows where Arnold is now, off to bigger and better things, I hope. But wherever he is, he is most likely working the veil for new possibilities.

A Chorus of Calls

I was deeply touched by the people I interviewed for this book—evocateurs and provocateurs and those answering the calls of the marketplace and the family and the routine. They offered up their deepest, most honest thoughts about their lives, intentions, and hopes as they allowed themselves to be challenged about how the sense of their callings worked out in their lives. They had a sense of the veil being lifted and worked at points in their lives and had committed, to a person, to being on the deep side of the veil as often as possible.

None of them pretended to have many answers, but they all had a story of their own to tell. Most, not all, had been responding to calls for a long time, at least five years. Some sensed that they had come to calls too late in their lives, and wished that they had started earlier. All had attracted helpers and most had attracted hinderers, evocateurs and saboteurs.

There was no arrogance in any of their voices, but there was a strong sense of joy and there were bouts with doubts and a sense of incompleteness. Some were bashful about the word *calling*.

Let's end our journey by listening to them talk about calls in their lives.

Tommye Wealand talks about finding models:

A key for me was finding the kind of role model I felt comfortable accepting. For the early part of my career I did not know any "successful" people who balanced head and heart. As a heart leader I fought what one boss told me: "Tommye, if you want to be successful you have to get 10 percent tougher every year." I abhorred that thought. In fact, my response to that was "I don't want to be successful if that's the price I have to pay."

Patrick Kelly, CEO, phrased the inevitability of the call in his life: "I knew it was possible, knew I had the talent. It would be stupid not to use it."

Sandy Smith, already identified as consultant and executive coach, is also the former COO of a large software concern. She talked about her slow discovery: "I'm sort of backing into the idea that I am living my calling. I've been intentional about how I live my life and choose my work but the idea I'm living my calling is recent."

Jan Ballard, Californian devoted to transforming the accounting profession, talked about the help he received, and the service message he absorbed: "I did most of my call discovery on my own, but I had many mentors, and my Dad told me one Easter that I would experience satisfaction in life to the degree I was able to be of service to my fellow human beings."

Dave Quammen, or Q, the writer and my old friend, also accepted help along the way, even the well-disguised kind:

Nobody ever hindered me. I had Irish luck all the way. Even the cruel brusque editors who rejected my bad and so-so work at the beginning, pointing me through years of dues and bartending, were doing me a great favor. I was extremely lucky to have friends, patrons, helpers, and partisans early on—just enough to get me marginally launched—and equally lucky that I didn't have massive, Roman-candle early success . . . because that only scrambles a person's brain and expectations, and makes it harder to tack into the world's cool headwind ever after.

Steve Sheppard of Foldcraft talked about calls specific and broad that intertwine:

I believe everyone has a calling and that it is our individual responsibility to seek it out. That means introspection, self-criticism, objective self-evaluation, and having the courage to follow whatever that direction may be. The lucky ones may end up exactly where we are meant to be. But I think that there is a broader call that exists for us too. It is this: wherever we may find ourselves, we have a call to make a difference, to create a positive impact on others, to make the world (our little corner of it) somehow better. . . . No matter what one's occupation or circumstances. Where the two "callings" meet, and feed each other, true inspiration and magic can occur.

If you are interested in what people you know have to say about their experience with calls, I have put the questions I used for my interviews in the appendix at the back of this book. Use them and make up your own. It is quite inspiring to get people who have Arnold's sense of working the veil to tell you how they do it and how they think about their calls.

WELCOMING YOUR CALLS WITH BALANCE

Answering a series of calls over our lifetimes will sanctify our lives and exalt our existence. A life is to be lived, a job is to be worked, a role is to be fulfilled. But a calling is something to become worthy of, to make a commitment to, to go on an extended journey for. A calling is like the bugle sounding at a great coronation—the notes ring out above the crowd and draw our attention to the highest of intentions and human possibilities.

It is for good reason that the last word is about two errors we can make when answering a call that we know is inherently uplifting. Let me re-remind you of two extremes:

We take the call too seriously and believe that we are above ordinary life and temptation.

We take the call too seriously and believe we are not worthy of such a lofty state of being.

The first mistake leads to the great sins of the ego that we see played out by those who set themselves above the rules. The calling they feel gets distorted into an ego-serving display of poor judgment, lack of empathy for others, and arrogance. "I have a calling, so I am somehow above the rules, which are for the little people anyway, don't you know. Now where can my limousine take me next?"

But the second mistake is equally damaging. If we feel unworthy of the calling we may shirk our duty, let fear keep us from getting on with the work, and choose ordinary life over extraordinary purpose. We may talk ourselves into being pragmatic and realistic—"Now I'd better get back to the stuff of my job, and leave my illusions of making a difference to another lifetime"—rather than give it our best shot and seek a unique way to express our real voice.

The first error is one of inflation and self-promotion and the second of deflation and self-protection.

Answering your call takes a balance of humility and boldness, sincerity without somberness, direction mixed with doubt. It is an adventure of human intent and heavenly grace. Answering your call invites this grace into your life. In the words of Scott Peck, author of *The Road Less Traveled*, "While we cannot will ourselves to grace, we can by will open ourselves to its miraculous coming. We can prepare ourselves to be fertile ground. A welcoming place."[1]

Listen intently for and welcome your calls. Answer them with all the might and love, wisdom and cleverness, heart and passion you can muster. Then lighten up, take a walk, plant your garden, work a crossword puzzle, and read the funnies. Act now, and know that the call will still be there in the morning.

Growing at Ease with the Hidden Depths

Demand of yourself that you live on the other side of the veil to experience the essence of life. Practices like looking past behavior to intention, assuming the yearning even in those who have forgotten why they are here, framing your actions and those of others in meaningful terms—all help the humdrum aspects of life take on deeper significance.

Remember the words and experiences of others, the millions of others who are on their path and mustering up the ideas and spunk to get on with their calls.

Enjoy the magnificence of calls and what they bring to your life and the lives of others, while keeping the perspective that the magnificence is reserved for your higher self and its call and not your ego and its role-bound day-to-dayness. Our long lives allow for commonality sprinkled with heroism, routine laced with rarefied spirit.

EXERCISE: WORKING THE VEIL

- How can I work the veil in all my activities to find the deeper life at my doorstep?
- What conversations could I be having with those around me to provoke more meaning and intention? What questions need I ask? What listening could I be doing?
- What role am I in that has deeper dimensions if I call it forth and evoke what lies beneath? My job? My parenting? My neighboring?
- What mission statement in my company have I ignored? Could I read it as a legitimate statement of highest intent? Can't I commit to my own mission statement for my work?
- How have I let my cynicism, laziness, or lack of imagination get in the way of seeing what is possible?

PART III

Summary

Although discovering your calls and learning to respond to them have their charm and hold the delight of the new, only staying focused for the long term can bring a life of callings well heeded and well lived. The long-term proposition of managing the energy and the tricks of the ego and of working the veil to see beneath the routines you face are two of the most important skills in answering your call.

Living a dual existence—like a counterspy—is what the long term takes. Because none of us float off into sainthood once we get moving on our calls, the real world of making money, using our egos, and establishing our roles never goes away. Thank God for that. This life is more interesting than the clouds, at least for the time being.

But the other side of the veil is what our egos and roles can't get us, and our dual existence also requires us to live in service and from our essence, to be impractical and to forget about money and our roles even while we attend to them.

How perplexingly cool is that?

Damned if we opt for only one existence, one side of the veil; saved if we opt for both.

We are summoned to figure this tricky duality out and live it enough to avoid making a mess of our lives and to contribute in the fashion we best can. That way we can step into the largeness of our journey and share its grace with others.

Appendix

Questions in Interviews for Answering Your Call

I prefaced the interview questions as follows. Some people I asked face-to-face and some by email. This note was used in emails; I paraphrased in the face-to-face encounters:

> I am writing a book about callings, why it is that people are drawn to do the things they do, not building careers necessarily, although that contains much for many of us, but adding value to the world in some way. So I am contacting some of the intentional people I know, for interviews, or if you would prefer, to email me back with responses to the following questions.
>
> Some don't like the term *calling* and that is OK—it is not a fit for everyone. But most find it workable. If you could send me a page or two on what you think of as you pursue what makes meaning for you, I'd really appreciate it. And who knows, you may be forever memorialized through the book.
>
> Thanks for the consideration.
>
> John

The Questions

1. When did you first realize you had a calling? How else would you phrase this calling phenomenon for you, if at all?
2. Who helped you discover you call . . . or did you do most of it on your own?
3. How did they help you?
4. Who hindered you on your journey to live out what you perceived as your calling? (No names most likely, but roles and instances would be helpful.)
5. What did you do and how did you overcome them?
6. What form has the calling taken over the years; how did it change as your life expanded and you matured?
7. When do you know you are answering your call?
8. When do you know you are not answering it so well?
9. Do you doubt your call at times? Wish it would go away? Wonder if you have read it right all these years?
10. Any other thoughts?

Notes

Introduction

1. Doris Lessing, *Briefing for a Descent into Hell* (New York: Vintage Books, 1981), p. 127.
2. See Frederic Hudson, *Adult Years* (San Francisco: Jossey-Bass, 1991).
3. This list represents some of my thoughts on books, authors, or categories of books not used for calling work, but which I think have merit. They may be overlooked, not in general, but as related to calls and our responses to them. I am not listing any of the books with callings in the title, not because they are not worth listing but because you can easily find them.

    Reading about calls lived over a lifetime is one of my favorite sources for seeing calls at work. David McCullough's biographies of Truman (New York: Simon & Schuster, 1992) and John Adams (New York: Simon & Schuster, 2001) are two I've read with joy. But Nelson Mandela's life, Eleanor Roosevelt's, and many more are rich sources in seeing calls working their ecstasy and demanding their response with relentless insistence. One of the first I read was about international civil servant Ralph Bunche. One caution: most biographies are about famous people and you can end up making the calls-are-for-big-people mistake.

    Peter Block's *The Answer to How Is Yes* (San Francisco: Berrett-Koehler, 2001) offers his usual provocative insight into how intensely our culture and parts of our consciousness conspire against callings; it is Thoreau's *Walden Pond* updated and psychologized. Parker Palmer's *Let Your Life Speak: Listening for the Voice of Vocation* (San Francisco: Jossey-Bass, 1999) is fine Palmer writing and has a great section on dealing with depression as part of the journey. Victor Frankl's *Man's Search for Meaning* (London: Beacon Press, 2000) may be the all-time classic for being called in horrific surroundings. (I heard him speak in person when I was nineteen.) *Chained to the Desk* by Bryan Robinson (New York: NYU Press, 2001) reminds us that workaholics suffer from selves that are squelched and the subsequent substitution of poor work strategies for callings. On the fiction side, read any edition of J.R.R. Tolkien's *Lord of the Rings*. Frodo is one called hobbit dude.

Chapter 1

1. Lily Tomlin, *The Search for Intelligent Life in the Universe* (New York: HarperCollins, 1986).
2. Kierkegaard. For more on Kierkegaard, go to www.webcom.com/kierke/.
3. David Quammen, *Song of the Dodo* (New York: Scriber's, 1997).
4. Francis Thompson, "The Hound of Heaven" (www2.bc.edu /~anderso/sr/ft.html).

Chapter 3

1. Michael Downey, *Trappist: Living in the Land of Desire* (New York: Paulist Press, 1997), p. 140.
2. Downey, *Trappist,* p. 140.

Chapter 4

1. Ken Kesey, *One Flew Over the Cuckoo's Nest* (New York: New American Library, 1989).

Chapter 6

1. Gary Hamel, *Leading the Revolution* (Boston: HBR Press, 2000), p. 4.
2. Betsy Harvey Kraft, *Mother Jones: One Woman's Fight for Labor* (Clarion Books, 1995).
3. S. Johnathan Bass, *Blessed Are the Peacemakers: Martin Luther King, Jr., Eight White Religious Leaders and the "Letter from Birmingham Jail."* (Baton Rouge: Louisiana State University Press, 2002).
4. Jeff Gates, *Democracy at Risk* (Cambridge, Mass.: Perseus Publishing, 2000), p. 243.
5. Bass, *Blessed Are the Peacemakers.*
6. Gifford Pinchot, *Intrapreneuring: Why You Don't Have to Leave the Corporation to Become an Entrepreneur* (New York: HarperCollins, 1985/San Francisco: Berrett-Koehler, 1999); Gifford Pinchot with Libby Pinchot, *The Intelligent Organization* (San Francisco: Berrett-Koehler, 1994); Hamel, *Leading the Revolution.*
7. "The Mad Farmer Revolution" from *Collected Poems 1957–1982* by Wendell Berry. Copyright © 1985 by Wendell Berry. Reprinted by permission of North Point Press, a division of Farrar, Straus and Giroux, LLC.

Chapter 7

1. C. S. Lewis, *The Screwtape Letters* (San Francisco: HarperCollins, 2001).
2. For more on Reinhold Niebuhr, see www.leaderu.com/isot/docs/niehbr3.html.

Chapter 8

1. M. Scott Peck, *The Road Less Traveled,* 2nd ed. (New York: Touchstone Books 1998), p. 308.

Index

I

identity, 84
"I Have a Dream" (King), 132
The Intelligent Organization (Pinchot), 104
internal focus, 29
Intrapreneuring: Why You Don't Have to Leave the Corporation to Become an Entrepreneur (Pinchot), 104
intrapreneurs, 93

J

Jones, Mother, 95–97
joy, 18–19
Joyce, James, 93
Jung, Carl, 1

K

kairotic time, 22–23, 133. *See also* depth level
Kelly, Patrick, 62, 137
Kennedy, Robert, 27–28
Kierkegaard, Søren, 18, 20, 120
King, Martin Luther, Jr., 91, 98, 101, 132
Koestenbaum, Peter, 45, 62

L

labor movement, 95–97
leadership, calls to, 32, 115
Leading the Revolution (Hamel), 104
Lessing, Doris, 3
"Letter from Birmingham Jail" (King), 101
Lewis, C. S., 115
life lie, 116

life roles. *See* roles
limitlessness. *See* expansiveness
The Lord of the Rings (Tolkien), 19–20

M

"The Mad Farmer Revolution" (Berry), 104–106
Mandela, Nelson, 93, 99, 102
Marcus Aurelius, 100–101
marketplace
    calls to, 31, 115
    provocateurs in, 93
Maslow, Abraham, 50
McClean, Pamela, 43–44
Mead, Margaret, 93
miracles, 50
monastery life, 47–48
Montessori, Maria, 94
Moore, Henry, 36
moral order, calls to, 32–33
multiple calls
    portfolio model, 27–29, 37
    and roles, 4–5
    vs. obvious calls, 4, 25–26
mystery, 6–7, 14, 36
mythologizing, 102

N

nature, calls to, 34
Niebuhr, Reinhold, 122
Nielsen, Harold, 83

O

One Flew Over the Cuckoo's Nest, 58–61
overwork, 68

About the Author

AT AGE TWENTY-FIVE, John Schuster's early trek into the world—first as a teacher in the inner city of Chicago and then as a youth advocate keeping troubled kids out of court in Cincinnati—came to an end. He then entered the developmental door that opened at the Environmental Protection Agency. He worked there for seven years, beginning his education in the world of large organizations and eventually serving as a director of human resources. He couldn't figure out how to use his master's degree in English yet, and he felt called to "see how society makes these big decisions to allocate resources to some human endeavors and not others" (one of his early journal entries).

At age thirty-two, having moved to Kansas City, he was single again with two sons to support, and he felt called to start his training and consulting practice. It was decision by default, innocence, and will—he couldn't think of anything better to do to use his talents, was clueless about running a business, and wanted to "go for it." He had no clients, no car, and $5,000 to carry him; he shared a studio apartment with a truck-driving buddy who was saving to go to chiropractic school. Having no car was a problem; in order to conduct one of his early seminars he had to take the bus to the location (this was Kansas City, not New York) and hitch a ride home with one of the participants.

Going out on his own was a precipitating event in his life. Schuster began his push into the American marketplace as a businessman and entrepreneur. His first mission statement from 1982 concluded with these words: "to help organizations develop to their fullest and to help individuals achieve more job and life satisfaction."

This phase of his calling took the form of workshops and speaking and consulting. He grew into leadership development work and into coaching CEOs on their businesses and their lives. His calling to spread the use of sound business practices and business literacy as a force for social good took him into pioneering the practices that became known as open-book management. Schuster and his colleagues developed tools and methods to help organizations engage their workforces by helping them understand their place in the business, providing them "line of sight" in workplaces that offered lots of feedback.

Today, he coaches leaders and teams, and speaks at large gatherings on living a called life and creating spirited workplaces. With his colleagues at the Schuster Kane Alliance, he assists companies that are serious about creating leadership and accountability across the organization through training and consulting.

Schuster teaches at Rockhurst University, the Jesuit school in Kansas City. He works locally and nationally, with occasional jaunts abroad. He plays sports and the guitar, gardens, and reads. He pays attention to calls, and yearns for a society that deploys its resources in ways that develop our humanity and our communities to their fullest. He feels called to participate wholeheartedly in the business he shares with his colleagues, in his family, and in his community. He has much to be happy about and even more to be humble about.

Other books by John Schuster are *Hum-Drum to Hot-Diggity: On Leadership* (Kansas City: Steadfast Publishers, 2000), *The Power of Open-Book Management* (New York: John Wiley, 1996), and *The Open-Book Management Fieldbook* (New York: John Wiley, 1998).

You can reach him at jschuster@skalliance.com, www.skalliance.com, or www.answeringyourcall.com.

Berrett-Koehler Publishers

Berrett-Koehler is an independent publisher of books, audios, and other publications at the leading edge of new thinking and innovative practice on work, business, management, leadership, stewardship, career development, human resources, entrepreneurship, and global sustainability.

Since the company's founding in 1992, we have been committed to creating a world that works for all by publishing books, periodicals, and other publications that help us to integrate our values with our work and work lives, and to create more humane and effective organizations.

To find out about our new books, special offers, free excerpts, and much more, subscribe to our **free monthly eNewsletter** at www.bkconnection.com.

Please see next pages for other publications from Berrett-Koehler Publishers

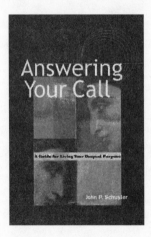